In the Image of God

In the Image of God

A Psychoanalyst's View

STANLEY A. LEAVY

Routledge
Taylor & Francis Group
New York   London

First published by Lawrence Erlbaum Associates, Inc. Publishers
10 Industrial Avenue
Mahwah, New Jersey 07430

Reprinted 2009 by Routledge

Routledge

270 Madison Avenue
New York, NY 10016

2 Park Square, Milton Park
Abingdon, Oxon OX14 4RN, UK

Originally published in 1988 by Yale University Press.
First paperback reprint 1997.

Library of Congress Cataloging-in-Publication Data

Leavy, Stanley A., 1915-
  In the image of God: a psychoanalyst's view / Stanley A. Leavy.
    p.   cm.
  Includes index.
  ISBN 0-88163-276-7
  1. Man (Christian theology) 2. Image of God. 3 > Psychoanalysis and religion. I.
Title

BT702.L42 1988   87-36770
235'.5-dc19

                                           CIP

10 9 8 7 6 5 4 3 2 1

In grateful memory of my parents,

JOSEPHINE AND NATHAN

Man thus created is man as the image of God. He is the image of God not in spite of but just because of his bodiliness. For in his bodiliness he is related to the earth and to other bodies, he is there for others, he is dependent upon others. In his bodiliness he finds his brother and the earth. As such a creature man of earth and spirit is in the likeness of his Creator, God.

DIETRICH BONHOEFFER

Contents

Introduction:
Imago Dei

When I was a very young man considering a medical career, I discovered a little book by an English physician that has stayed with me for more than a half century; the same old "Everyman" volume, much underlined, remains on my desk. It was Thomas Browne's *Religio Medici*, a work perhaps best known as a curiosity of seventeenth-century English literary style. Its famous Latinisms appealed to the classicist that I was in those days, and the late mediaeval atmosphere of the book gave it the sharp, colorful outlines of stained glass. There was nothing static about it, however; it pointed again and again to the spiritual struggles of a traditional Christian believer in touch with the upheavals, spiritual and political, of a modern world. We find in Browne, on the whole, neither a reactionary defender of past summations of thought nor a progressive at odds with the European Christian heritage. In his dense rhetoric, with its organ tones and its curious harmonies, Browne presented the life of science as he knew it, infused with the many graces of his faith. When I visited the English cathedral town of Norwich some years ago, saw in the marketplace the seated statue of the old doctor, and in the church of St. Peter Mancroft looked across the nave at the memorial plaque that marks his grave, I resolved that if I were to offer my view of humanity, as psychoanalyst and Christian, I would have *Religio Medici* in mind. This, then, like Browne's, is a personal meditation and no more an epitome of psychoanalysis than the *Religio* is of medicine.

I do not wish to exaggerate my affinities with Thomas Browne. Most obviously, he was not born a Jew as I was, and his allusions to my people are the customary ones of an Englishman of his time—at best condescending. He also gave the superstitions of his time more credence than they deserved; as a judge, he condemned witches to death. He wrote his book when his "pulse had not beat thirty years," whereas I write mine in my seventies. To try to write like him would be simultaneously grandiose and absurd. Where I do claim to follow him is mainly in the conviction that the intensified study of nature—in my case, human nature—leads toward and not away from faith in God. In Browne's words:

> The whole Creation is a Mystery, and particularly that of Man. At the blast of His mouth were the rest of the Creatures made, and at His bare word they started out of nothing: but in the frame of Man (as the Text describes it,) He played the sensible operator, and seemed not so much to create, as make him. When He had separated the materials of other creatures, there consequently resulted a form and a soul: but, having raised the walls of Man, He was driven to a second and harder creation of a substance like Himself, an incorruptible and immortal Soul.[1]

To the skeptical mind, it has always seemed more than a little ludicrous that human beings, odd enough when they believe in God, go still further and profess to resemble him, to be made of "a substance like Himself." Don't they rather make a God in their own image? No one would question that the ancient gods and goddesses of Homer resemble humans; indeed, they are all too human, and that is one reason they were forsaken.

But the claim in Genesis is that the mysterious One—who summoned up light in the everlasting darkness, and made earth and sun and moon and stars, and was utterly unlike any of the members of the Olympian family—created humans "in His own image."[2] That is, this creature that so rapidly fell from the state of grace bears in himself, in some all-important way, the likeness of the One whose name cannot even be uttered.

There is never a convincing answer to the skeptic, except perhaps to remind him or her that the act of questioning, of refusing to submit to received opinion, may, when it is not undertaken out of mere prudence or contrariness, itself be exemplary of the image of God in man. For, as many philosophers and theologians since St. Augustine have said, it is in transcending ourselves and extending our consciousness beyond the immediately given that we show our humanity.[3] We make the world, and our own nature, the object of our knowledge. To attempt to understand our world, to look for meaning in it, to add to the creation, and above all, perhaps, to make it the object of loving concern—these actions correspond with the picture of God that has been revealed to us. All we can do is to invite the skeptic to join us in the actions that we believe we perform in God's likeness, omitting or maybe just postponing the specifically *religious* act—worship of God.

That our likeness to God was damaged by some original disobedience seems to be a common tenet of Christian theology. I take it that this view is not fully shared by Judaism, which holds that the "fall" brought on punishment enough, but did not so alter human nature that a suffering redeemer was needed to restore it. It either case, even the blindest optimist would be hard put to find in human nature as we know it an unmodified representation of the best that we could hope for. The *imago dei* that abides in us would seem to be more an aspiration than a present fulfillment.

Still, within a Christian frame, it is incumbent on the student of psychoanalysis to presume that any person is indeed made in God's image, "warts and all"—that is, to accept that the disfigurements are not ultimately alienating. This conviction encourages us to believe that people can move toward more satisfying lives, insofar as they are able to transcend the present state of their world. The *imago dei* may never be realizable as such, but as a symbol of the implicit human life-project, it holds out hope.

For the psychoanalyst, the word *imago* has another and more familiar interest. It has fallen out of favor (along with C. G. Jung, who first applied it in our field), although it is a strictly psychoanalytic concept and frequently appears under other names.[4] Imagos in this sense are unconscious prototypes or representations of the members of one's family. Fixed in the distortions of the remote past, they not only affect our present relations with family members but orient our relations with others. We refer naturally enough to a "father-imago" or "mother-imago." The concept is strained a little in the form of "God-imago"; nevertheless, it is worthwhile to juxtapose the two aspects of the *imago dei*: on the one hand, the likeness to God that we owe to our creator; on the other hand, the likeness of our creator that we hold, often unbeknownst, in our minds. The latter imago is likely to remain under the sovereignty of parental imagos that are difficult to dispel, and therein lies much of our unbelief, for all its masking in the glorious iconography of the Middle Ages and the Renaissance.

Thomas Browne's example stands me in further good stead. He was no theologian, nor am I. He assumed that as a believer he could "collect Divinity" not only from the sacred Scriptures but also from "the Book of . . . Nature, that universal and publick Manuscript, that lies expans'd unto the Eyes of all."[5] If scientific knowledge of nature did not belong to the believer's grasp of reality, we would have to cling to a narrow cosmology based on the biblical myths (as Browne had to do before the scientific revolution was well under way), blinding ourselves to the richness and complexity of the world—the *creation*, as we have come to understand it. That man is a created being is no less a matter of faith for believers now than it was for Browne in pre-

Darwinian days. That some religious people, and all atheists, consider the evolutionary hypothesis incompatible with a belief in creation is a measure of their lack of imagination.

Like Browne, I hold that the deliberate study of the operations of the mind must yield results that are not just compatible with religious faith but amplify it. The knowable internal and external relations of our minds are part of the creation and thus, in their special way, open to scrutiny. The belief that our minds transcend the world in the act of contemplating it, as Augustine taught, should in no way limit the scope of psychological understanding. I hold that the Freudian psychoanalysis I have learned and practiced reveals valuable insights into the "image of God" as it takes shape in individual lives. While the findings of psychoanalysis are less precise and conclusive than those of natural science, they add up to a true and rational picture. This is the way the human creation works.

The following chapters were first presented as brief lectures for discussion by a church audience of educated men and women. The group included another psychoanalyst, several psychotherapists, and a number of other professionals, lay and clerical. Because I intended to speak as clearly as I could to those who were not technically trained in analytic thought, I kept close to ordinary language. It is always an open question how fully we can impart concepts when they are separated from the words in which they have traditionally been cast. I took the risk of being misunderstood through oversimplification, in preference to the equal risk of veiling my meaning in a specialized language. I have, however, taken advantage of the opportunity afforded by publication to add comments and excursuses where they seemed desirable. I hope that these annotations will be of use to readers whose curiosity is aroused by my assertions and contentions, but the earlier statements, slightly modified, should stand on their own.

I have kept to a minimum any apologetic stance with regard to religious belief and practice. This may appear remarkable in a psychoanalytic work, but it should not be. While atheist writers may contribute to our understanding of religion, it is rather in the way that celibates may help us understand sexuality; neither ought to have the last word. Under the circumstances of my original lectures, it was hardly necessary to defend religion. Addressing what I hope will be a larger audience, I bear in mind that tenets and experiences familiar to men and women who meet together regularly for liturgical worship often strike others as very peculiar indeed. While I think that I understand their perplexity, I can only assure them that these lines were written with conviction but with no pretensions to unique truth. If anyone is encouraged by what I have written to make religious inquiry, I urge him or her to look further, to "come and see." There are many churches and synagogues, and few are overcrowded.

Some question is bound to arise about my own religious affiliation. I have already indicated my beginnings in Judaism. For most of my life I have been a Christian, and for the past forty years, roughly corresponding with my time as a student and then practitioner of psychoanalysis, a member of the Anglo-Catholic (Episcopal) parish where these lectures were given. No doubt this complexity of spiritual development has left its strains; it has also been an advantage in permitting me to understand at first hand many things that "cradle-Christians" are apt to ignore. At all events, I am grateful to the religion I came from and to the one that I found awaiting me.

My talks were presented at the invitation of Frs. Jerald Miner and Donnel O'Flynn of Christ Church in New Haven. I wish to thank them for inspiring this book in more ways than one. I am also under obligation to all the faithful attenders on Sunday mornings, and especially to Susan and Timothy Bingham, whose audiotapes of the talks were of exceptional assistance when I came to put them into the present form. Jane and Richard Lewis, Jungian analysts, read my brief discussion of Jung, and while not in full agreement with my interpretations did not discern factual errors. My wife, Margaret, in addition to being the best of listeners, took time unstintingly from her own writing to make mine better. Gladys Topkis, my editor at Yale University Press, has admirably combined patience with insistence, and Harry Haskell has made many useful emendations.

Notes

1. Thomas Browne, *Religio Medici* (1642; London: Dent, 1906), p. 40.
2. Genesis 1:26, 27 and 9:6.
3. See Reinhold Niebuhr, *The Nature and Destiny of Man* (New York: Scribner's, 1941), chap. 6.
4. See s.v. "Imago" in J. Laplanche and J. B. Pontalis, *The Language of Psychoanalysis* (New York: Norton, 1973).
5. *Religio Medici*, p. 17.

· I ·

Psychoanalyzing

Many ways are open to explore the human mind, and every explorer discovers a new world. So various is human nature that we cannot expect that it will be revealed identically to any two who search it out. Every new program of study will set itself different goals and follow different avenues of research. Furthermore, every student will pursue the phenomena of mind according to his or her own predisposition. An adventure in exploration of the mind is a solitary one, proceeding where no one has trodden before, because every life has been led differently, rising out of the "dark backward" of the womb and infancy and thrown into a world not of its own making or choosing. Consequently, generalizations about the mind are highly artificial and have to be adapted to individual cases. If that were the limit of our knowledge, our situation would be even more troublesome than it is, for we could never have any expectations in common with our fellows, let alone be able to agree on any psychology—that is, on any shared approach to studying the mind. We are not as restricted as that because we are willing to adopt some common programs of study and to pursue them by common methods. Every mind is unique, and we cannot travel together as though advancing up some mysterious river in the jungle or walking in the footsteps of Neil Armstrong on the moon. Nevertheless, by my favorite metaphor, we are explorers who have learned to use approximately the same maps.

As in all human enterprises, we can agree on some principles to follow in making the journey. Humankind abhors chaos, necessarily and universally, and always seeks order in existence. My world is not yours, but at the very least we share some ordering in time and space. Whoever has studied mental illnesses knows that people who do not share those categories become very hard to live with. They may ignore temporal routines entirely and never be where they are expected, or turn night into day and day into night. They may disregard the boundaries of property and privacy. In their presence we have thrust on us how great is our dependence on the conventional rules of order that govern our lives, individually and in community. Even "flower children" of recent memory had to make conventions of their own so as not to infringe on rights that they might have denied in principle.

The student of human nature presupposes much more than these elementary rules of society. As a matter of fact, we have a great organizing system that immediately establishes the boundaries of our examination—language. To discover anything about human nature, we need eventually to talk to one another. To be sure, some psychologists have based their methods on work done with animals, who cannot speak; their studies of human "behavior" have yielded interesting and sometimes surprising results, especially as long as their subjects keep their mouths shut. But when we learn only about what men and women "do", and not what they think and feel, we cannot hope for better than an impoverished story; indeed, they have no story at all if they do not tell us anything in words.[1]

So a psychoanalyst's view of human nature is derived from listening to stories told in a shared language, under a set of conditions that provide the elements of a common world. I refer to such fixed elements as agreed-upon times, place, and cost of the patient's treatment, but the common language is of primary importance. It is exceedingly difficult to carry on an analysis in an unfamiliar language, in which at best every nuance is lost in approximations. Some of the German-speaking psychoanalysts who introduced the method to America and England had remarkable gifts for the use of their adopted tongue; others—and accordingly their patients—were less fortunate. But more subtle differences exist within a common national language. Local and class influences affect usage of words, tonal expressions, the gestures that accompany or punctuate words, and so on. A further subtlety may underlie very deep difficulties in mutual understanding—namely, the purely personal values of words that depend on one's own history.

In truth, psychoanalysis is based on two conventions. One is the language shared by the analyst and his patient; the other is the theory espoused by the community of analysts. This theory is a way of observing, classifying, organizing, and summarizing what analysts hear. It purports to tell how the separate items we discover are causally related to one another. As in any scientific effort, we would not have looked for these items in the first place if we had no theory uniting them into a larger whole, but the theory must be elastic enough to leave room for the inevitable exceptions that every patient presents. Theories exist to enable us to see the woods as well as the trees. Yet it is not necessary or even likely that only one theory can be true. Were it not for my experience, I would find it hard to believe that men and women who have studied human nature for many years can conclude that a definitive theory is possible, let alone that it already exists. My own conviction is that analysts will always have many theoretical systems of interpreting human experience as it is reported to us. On the other hand, it is equally sure that not all the theories of mind nor all the available methods of treating mental suffering, will be of equal validity; it is not easy for the seeker after help or truth to know where to turn. I suggest that, coming from diverse points of departure, we must work together to improve our rules for evidence and examine our standards of competence in applying them. Above all, perhaps, we require a degree of openness to listen to one another's theories. It is not out of place here to take a lesson from the history of the doctrines of the church. Divisions arose out of understandable differences or reactions to errors, real or supposed. Often, however, they became so enshrined in borrowed holiness as to be closed to further question, making schism and enmity the consequence of what was supposed to be a better witness to revealed truth. Unfortunately, there is no reason to expect that we disciples of Freud will do a better job than the people of God in tolerating honest disagreement.[2]

Psychoanalysts have been schooled in the theory of the mind that Freud began propounding around a century ago and modified extensively in the course of his lifetime. It was devised in the first place to facilitate the treatment of suffering people, and to a great extent that is what psychoanalysis remains. Since Freud's death in 1939, the theory has been further modified by his followers, who are, as we have seen, by no means of one accord in their theoretical positions. Psychoanalysis as a whole is only one of many theories of the mind current in our century, perhaps the most famous one because it initially seemed to defy much of received opinion. Its opposition to traditional points of view, especially in religion and morals, may have helped it achieve a succès de scandale in quarters where its positive values were less apparent. I have practiced Freudian psychoanalysis throughout my professional life in a way similar to what Freud taught, although I have not shared some aspects of his theories, much less what I take to be his prejudices. I have held to the general program of psychoanalytic explanation without always coming to Freud's conclusions (an autonomy that I share with many of my colleagues). Psychoanalysis is a rare science in that one man's discoveries have had such a lasting impact. Although the name of Einstein comes up most often in popular discussion of modern physics, several other scientists—Planck, Dirac, Bohr, Heisenberg—are acknowledged to have similar rank. But no other psychoanalyst has rivaled the influence that Freud continues to exert nearly fifty years after his death. It is too easy to dismiss our respect as idolatry (which it sometimes is); the truth of the matter is that Freud's genius and energy drove him to a nearly universal inquiry into the workings of the mind, and that his ideas continue to stimulate new researches.[3]

The general program of psychoanalysis holds, to begin with, that when a person speaks, he or she always says more—and often something quite different—than is consciously intended. The situation in psychoanalysis is deliberately designed to make such double or unintended messages more readily available. The patient is asked to speak freely, not to withhold anything purposely, and preferably (in order to make this freedom easier) to lie in a relaxed position on a couch with the analyst out of sight behind him. In this way, the patient abandons much of the control that we normally exert over thoughts and speech and that ordinary conversation requires. Naturally, it is difficult for some to learn this unfamiliar mode of speaking; every patient has to accept "on faith" at first that it might be advantageous to think to no purpose. Disparaging comments (not sparing the analyst), business or personal confidences, dreams, religious and racial antipathies, embarrassing memories, sexual irregularities, or just intimacies not ordinarily narrated to others—all these make the process called "free association" difficult. Besides, patients in analysis at times have an overwhelming preference to talk only about the troubles that caused them to search for help.[4]

What is the purpose of this dubious freedom from inhibition? Is psychoanalysis a species of confession, related to the sacrament of penance? Although it does not include anything at all like the methodical listing of offenses recommended by priests to penitents, psychoanalysis does resemble penance, because no life is lived without infractions of some code of right and wrong. Feelings of guilt are relieved by telling the causes to a noncondemning ear, and the patient, like the penitent, feels at least temporarily restored to harmony with the community from which he or she had felt alienated. Simultaneously, the analyst, like the priest, learns many things about human nature that can

psychoanalysis is similar to penance

patient = penitent

analyst = priest

be applied generally. In time, both analysts and confessors come to be good listeners because they have "heard everything" and are no longer surprised by the curious things their fellow humans do, think, and say—if their own lives and experience of analysis have not already healthily disillusioned them.

But obtaining confessions is of very limited usefulness in psychoanalysis. One might say that psychoanalysis begins where confession to a priest ends, although the reverse is also true, since absolution in the religious sense is not to be looked for in psychoanalysis. An analyst, believer or not, does not as such represent the sacred being against whom the confessed offense is ultimately directed and from whom forgiveness comes. Further, an analyst is not so called because he hears secrets or even because he is understanding, learned, or an expert on sexuality. Analysts are able to interpret the unconscious meaning of what patients tell them—that is, to discern intentions of which the speaker was not aware. This is a rather specialized ability, one that is not even potentially present in many who might aspire to treat patients and that demands extensive training of those who do possess it. While the interpretation of dreams—especially his own dreams—was Freud's original "royal road to the unconscious" and remains an invaluable procedure today, it is only one of several means of access that the analyst must possess to hear the unconscious intentions in the stories told by the patient.

Why is it of use to interpret what has been unconscious? We all go through our lives living out intentions of which we are unaware at least as much as intentions that we recognize. A desire to get ahead in the world, to be "successful", is natural enough, since success carries with it possibilities of pleasure, security, prestige, and freedom that lack of success does not. On the other hand, the desire for success may obscure another intention. This can make it difficult if not impossible to achieve our goals—for instance, to surpass the brother who outdistanced us in childhood, as a student or athlete, or won unmerited praise from our parents. Such intentions, based on lifelong jealousy, may have remained hidden or been treated as of little importance, because it would be painful, shameful, or depressing to acknowledge them. Recognizing such intentions is by no means easy; they may have entered into all sorts of other motives and become involved with a host of one's human relations. We might say that keeping them in the dark has been a major business of one's mind. Clues to these intentions can often be picked up very gradually, as the analyst detects in words and phrases—and some actions, too—particular allusions that are at variance with more evident subjects. In the unconscious struggle of the man with his brother, the hidden intention might have come to light through mention of those fairy tales of Grimm in which the youngest child is specially favored, so that the analyst eventually exposes the patient's hidden fantasy of becoming the favored one and triumphing over the wicked siblings or giants. In reality, this outcome might amount to little more than becoming rich or influential socially or academically, but as long as the secret desire remains unfulfilled, the success remains ungratifying. An unconscious childhood fantasy, holding a foothold in consciousness through the mediation of the Grimm story, has governed too much of a person's life.[5]

When I evaluate the important and enduring in Freud's discoveries, I place the active unconscious at the top. We need to consider the consequences of that role. If whatever we say or think—and, by the same token, whatever we do—is not only what we consciously intend but also the vehicle of purposes that we did not know we had, then it is as if we were inhabited by another personality in addition to the one we habitually present to ourselves and the world. The question of responsibility immediately comes to mind, as it has since Freud first put forth his theories of the workings of the mind.[6] If my actions are dictated by forces over which I have no control, whose actions are they? In other forms, this is hardly a new idea. St. Paul said something of the sort when he lamented doing the things he ought not to do and failing to do the things he ought to do, as if he, too, were reflectively aware that he acted, or failed to act, unconsciously.[7] Even if he meant only that he quite consciously yielded to temptations too strong to withstand, the implication is that the act of yielding was against his will.

One of Freud's earliest ways of presenting the idea of unconscious motivation was as "counter-will" (*Gegenwille*), a word that is worth keeping in mind whenever we say "the unconscious."[8] Will, so rich in philosophical overtones, has been played down by psychoanalysis. Being a verb as well as a noun, the word *will* always implies a subject. When I do something that I claim I didn't want to do, that I didn't will, my listener has the right to ask, as any analyst might, "Who, then, did want to?" The answer must be that I did. It does no good to plead that blind, impersonal, unconscious forces "did" the act: they are me. But it is equally incorrect, we learn from psychoanalysis, to assume that all our actions are willed in the same way. We may ask, paraphrasing Spinoza: "It is true that I can do what I will, but can I will what I will?"[9] The aspect of the "I" that—or who—enforces my willing is hard to grasp. In psychoanalysis we try to reveal that other will and to be brave enough to acknowledge it as our own. Paul, no mean psychologist, is again helpful in reminding us of our inability to carry out the Law as he understood it.[10] I think that, faced with the psychoanalytic evidence of unconscious motivation and aware as he was of our unwillingness to acknowledge our helplessness, Paul would see yet another evidence of divine Grace in our owning up to the unconscious.

To set things in the right perspective, I must warn that Freud often put the matter in quite another fashion. Much of the time, he and his followers have thought of psychoanalysis as a natural science. One of the deepest convictions of natural scientists has been, until pretty recently, that they observe nature objectively. The ideal of scientific study was to be impersonal, free of the "human factor," and not to import subjective intentions into nature itself. There have been surprising alterations in these views in our century, especially among physicists, but psychoanalysis, as an attempt at natural science, was built on the foundations of an earlier science.[11] Freud did not stay with the "counterwill" but posited a personal unconscious powered by impersonal energies—"instincts" or "drives" (*Triebe*), as he called them.[12] This shift had the seeming merit of approaching the terminology of academic psychologists who work with animals (whose intention or "will" we can never know because animals do not tell stories), or better yet, the physicists and chemists whose methods permit them to differentiate, record, and measure the "energies" underlying the properties of physical forms.

Reading Freud, or hearing the lectures of some psychoanalysts, one must not be misled into believing that psychoanalysts have discovered impersonal and yet supposedly mental forces acting within human beings. It is true that we are not so free as we sometimes like to think, but the constraints on our freedom—aside from those imposed by our biological structure and our society—are derived from our history and are therefore of our own making. Our personal history merits particular attention in that it is at the same time a constraint on our freedom and the source of it. What psychoanalysts know about human nature comes solely from the stories that patients have told us, and those stories are their histories.

In the following chapters, I propose to take up aspects of life on which psychoanalysis has something to tell us and to reflect on what this means to Christians and other believers. My subject is the "image of God" in humans or, more properly, the refractions of that image that psychoanalysts have gathered. I shall limit myself to observations that I can defend on the basis of my experience and that of colleagues whose work I trust, but I may not supply enough evidence to convince skeptics. Much of what psychoanalysts teach has passed into popular knowledge or belief without having undergone critical scrutiny. This has not been an unmixed blessing, since the experiences voiced by patients can be only sketchily encapsulated in generalizations about human nature, and we may convey the wrong impression as easily as the right one in our attempts to popularize psychoanalysis. If even as gifted a writer as Freud often failed to get his ideas across, how much worse lesser popularizers have done. Theoretical notions may serve not to enlighten so much as to darken understanding: the concept of the Oedipus complex, for example, is often used coarsely or incorrectly, rather than as the formula that illuminates the subtle interactions and passions of the family.

My own point of view as a psychoanalyst has moved from an eager reaching out for certainties about the mind to a philosophy of exploration by story telling and dialogue.[13] I have come to aim at having my patients "speak themselves" and in so doing to hear the contradictions, hidden longings, distortions, aspirations, expectations, and disappointments that long habits of mind have withheld from their consciousness. I have learned to draw on my own language, history, and imagination to further my effort to understand others. Like every analyst who has enjoyed his work, I have found psychoanalyzing a constant reminder of the inexhaustible variety of human nature, of how interesting, compassionate, creative, and alive—as well as how selfish, cruel, and tyrannical—human beings are.

I have divided this big subject into several topics pertinent to our study. What is usually called "development" I prefer to call "becoming," because of the psychoanalytic assumption that the past as it unfolds is always part of the present.[14] I want to look closely at loving and hating and suffering, which last is what brings people to become patients. The ways in which we conceal personal truth from ourselves is another subject that seems to me to have religious importance. Believing itself deserves the same kind of consideration as part of our existence. And I want to reflect on "ending," not only to ask questions about death and the life to come, but also to consider how the inevitability of dying affects our lives. These are not customary ways of discussing psychoanalysis, but I have the special purpose of trying to relate my life's work to the catholic Christian faith.

I take it as God's word that "the truth shall make you free," but without, I hope, arrogating to myself a monopoly of truth.

Notes

1. B. F. Skinner, perhaps the most eminent and certainly one of the most eloquent of behaviorists, accepts that "psychoanalysis is largely concerned with discovering and changing feelings." But being confined to observation to account for what happens, he understands the changes that take place in psychoanalysis to be exactly analogous to those that take place in experimental animals when physical rewards and punishments are applied. Oddly enough, Professor Skinner writes about feelings just as if he has them, too. Where he seems to differ radically from psychoanalysts and other students of the mind who respect reports of what people think and feel, is in his conviction that feelings, which he takes to be only physiological states, are not causally connected to the stories that are told by the people who feel them. See his "Outlining a Science of Feeling," in the *Times Literary Supplement* (London), 8 May 1987.

2. Theoretical differences that outsiders might consider "ideological," the kind that in religion are "doctrinal," sometimes undergo spontaneous resolution. The anathematized hypothesis turns out to have more in common with the "central" theory than we first thought possible. Much (some might say too much) of Alfred Adler's sociological influence has been absorbed by Freudian psychoanalysis, and part of the hitherto ridiculed account of infantile aggression propounded by Melanie Klein has come to sound better than plausible. Jacques Lacan described his exclusion from official psychoanalysis as an "excommunication" in that his former followers were forbidden by the international organization to have any further dealings with him when they returned to the parent group. But his influence has already pervaded the writings of French analysts, and it is likely that, separated from his contentious and often offensive personality, his radical criticism of psychoanalysis *from within* will continue to modify our thought.

3. For a masterly study of the operations of Freud's mind in the process of creating psychoanalysis, see *Freud's Self-Analysis* by Didier Anzieu, trans. Peter Graham (Madison, Conn.: International Universities Press, 1986).

4. A thorough examination of free association from a clinical point of view can be found in Anton Kris, *Free Association* (New Haven: Yale University Press, 1982).

5. This example may also stand for the importance of fairy tales, legends, myths, traditions, rituals and dreams (which they resemble in many respects) in the formation of unconscious mental structure. Their appeal to us, and especially to children, rests in their closeness to the primary

experiences of life as mediated through the childhood imagination. Frightening as they often are, they provide safe vehicles for the yet more frightening—because immediate—fantasies of childhood. Bruno Bettelheim has studied them extensively in *The Uses of Enchantment* (New York: Alfred A. Knopf, 1976).

6. Dreams are at once fully personal to us and totally alien from us. We have them entirely to ourselves, so that even in narrating them there is no possibility of corroborating their content or the intentions displayed in them. Furthermore, no one is entitled to hold that the dreamer dreamed otherwise than he or she claimed. Yet the dreamer, on waking, may find his intentions as well as the scene and actions of his dream foreign to waking life and thought. For all this fundamental contradiction, the dream is the dreamer's own. The analysis of dreams has as one of its purposes the discovery of the historical events and the intentions that the dream discloses, and their acknowledgment by the dreamer. In this sense, dreams are private fairy tales.

7. Romans 7:19. Paul follows this admission with the statement: "If I do that I would not, it is no more I that do it, but sin that dwelleth in me" (Authorized Version). This is not self-exculpatory, since "sin," in Paul's theology, is part of man's natural being, not to be excused as external.

8. Freud introduced the concept of "counter-will" in 1892, in his "Case of Successful Treatment by Hypnotism" (*The Standard Edition of the Complete Psychological Works of Sigmund Freud*, ed. James Strachey [London: Hogarth Press, 1953–74], vol. 1, p. 122; hereafter, *Standard Edition*). He described it as the source of an "antithetic idea," that is, an idea that was not present in the waking state of his patient but was functionally operative nonetheless and became apparent during hypnosis. This concept helped Freud to come to an understanding of hysterical attacks. In "The Mechanism of Hysterical Phenomena" (*Standard Edition*, vol. 3, p. 32), he said that a patient's "fear that she might make a noise turned into actually making one—an instance of 'hysterical counter-will.'" Freud turned to counter-will in his 1901 *Psychopathology of Everyday Life* (*Standard Edition*, vol. 6, p. 158n) to explain the mistakes and delays that often occur in making payments; elsewhere in the same work, Freud attributes many kinds of errors and omissions to the same origin. It is typical of Freud's remarkable capacity to draw unexpected generalizations from widely disparate phenomena that still later, in 1912, he introduced the counter-will as the "internal obstacle" to certain sufferers from sexual impotence (*Standard Edition*, vol. 11, p. 179). The term seems to disappear thereafter. Probably the generalization fell apart into concepts like resistance, repression, unconscious conflict, and ultimately, drive. But the gain in specificity was accompanied by the loss of the implication of a personal "will."

9. The affinity of Freudian thinkers for Spinoza is understandable. His

determinism takes mental life into account, and it is easy (whether or not it is correct) to grant metaphoric status to his theism, which is really pantheism. Spinoza's insight into the unconscious operation of the emotions is also strikingly similar, if in a highly abstract form, to that of psychoanalysis. He writes that "the more an emotion becomes known to us, the more it is within our power and the less the mind is passive to it" (*Ethics*, part 5, prop. 3, corollary). See also Lou Andreas-Salomé, *The Freud Journal*, trans. S. A. Leavy (New York: Basic Books, 1964), pp. 74–76.

10. Romans 8:3, 4.

11. To extend Heisenberg's uncertainty principle to psychoanalysis is a faulty analogy. The influence of the process of observation on the actions of subatomic particles sounds like, but probably has nothing to do with, the effects created by the analytic observer on the communications of patients. That the analyst must always cause a disturbance should be evident from the nature of dialogue and not require substantiation from physics.

12. James Strachey, the general editor of the *Standard Edition* of Freud's works, writes that the word "instinct" (*Trieb*) is "scarcely" to be found in Freud's writings before 1905, but "the instincts were of course there under other names." Some of these earlier synonyms, such as "affective ideas" and "wishful impulses," carry personal overtones; others, such as "excitations" and "endogenous stimuli," do not (*Standard Edition*, vol. 14, p. 114). However that may be, for the purposes of making a general theory, psychoanalysis has found it convenient, in using the idea of "instinct," to have a term in which the impersonal aspect predominates. We see a subtle but significant change in certain later analysts, notably H. W. Loewald, who wrote in 1972: "When I speak of instinctual forces and of instincts or instinctual drives, I define them as motivational, i.e., both motivated and motivating. . . . Instincts remain relational phenomena, rather than being considered energies within a closed system . . . " (*Papers on Psychoanalysis*, [New Haven; Yale University Press, 1980], pp. 152–53). With the introduction of the word "motive" and its related forms, we are in the human, personal world.

13. I have developed this theme in my *Psychoanalytic Dialogue* (New Haven: Yale University Press, 1980).

14. On the phenomenology of temporality in psychoanalysis, see H. W. Loewald, "The Experience of Time," in *Papers on Psychoanalysis*.

· 2 ·

Becoming

I have emphasized how analysts
depend on language and speech to do our work, the distinction
being between language, the common medium that we all share
and that provides a certain structure for our thinking, and
speech, which consists of separate or continuous acts of speaking. I said that almost all analysts know about anyone is what
he or she has told us, and that our method consists mainly of
story-telling and listening to stories.

Humans are not born speaking. The word *infant* means
"speech-less." Babies make sounds and it is out of those rudi-
mentary vocal expressions that speech and language come into
being; it is also likely that babies are "programmed" for language
through some arrangements in the nervous system.[1] But the acquisition of language occurs only in a milieu where there are
already speakers. A supposed test case of this proposition occurred in nineteenth-century France. The "wild boy" of Aveyron,
who apparently had lived from infancy by himself in the woods,
was brought into town, sheltered, and tutored; but he never
learned to speak and indeed could do little to care for himself
once away from the forest.[2] Learning to speak might be compared
to the process of watering a potted plant from below: just as

the water rises gently in the soil through capillary action, becoming more and more available to the tiny fibrous rootlets that absorb it, so the child is surrounded by a speaking environment for which it is prepared by the sense of hearing, by its own voice, by its visual imaging, and, not least, by the encouragement of loving attendants. We grow in a sea of speech and in a real sense only discover ourselves, and others, through speech.[3]

Nevertheless, we live a long time before we speak on our own; during that time we possess a powerful mental life. We know this only by inference; it would be mistaken to claim that we can know the preverbal child's mental life as we know his later, spoken life. We have to depend on what we observe in other ways than listening. However, preverbal modes of experience persist into later life and are subject to further study. It appears that babies increasingly single out perceptions from the overwhelming mass of sensations to which they are subjected. Their sensations and perceptions remain tied to external objects and actions. The infant "thinks," so to speak, in concrete images, sounds, tastes, smells, and feelings long before it does so in words. Wordless images drift into one another by proximities and similitudes. For example, the act of verifying that a window is not just the air that it reveals cannot take place lastingly before the acquisition of language. Concepts like window, glass, solid object, and impenetrability organize the experience of knowing that objects can exist without being visible themselves.

The point of these comments would be lost if I limited their intent to describing the role of language as an experience. To the contrary, I would emphasize that the earliest, nonverbal kinds of experience endure all our lives. Dreams, for example, present an inextricable fusion of life *before* language, and life *in* language. The images that we see in dreams are partly drawn from language, to the extent that they "symbolize," and partly from a more primitive stage of childish imagination, when they stand for the objects they represent and nothing more.[4]

All I have said so far about language—a subject to which I

shall return frequently—illustrates that human becoming is a constant thrust into the new, but never abandons its grasp of the past. We never entirely surpass our infancy. To some extent, we are always in touch with the wordless, helplessly dependent infants we once were. We even continue to call out with wordless cries when the world in which we find ourselves becomes incomprehensible, which may be rather often, if we are honest about it. If we look at the process of becoming as one in which the accumulation of experience and knowledge takes place alongside the physical changes of our bodies, we see that we are the product of our history, of our past, in all respects. Genetic and other biological structures must in some measure, often mysterious to us, govern our mental as much as our physical lives. From earliest infancy, individual differences have to be attributed to inborn dispositions that affect mental life at least as much as they are affected by it.[5]

So, too, growing up in one rather than another language affects how we think; we are formed by the whole cultural milieu that we take for granted, but which is by no means fixed. We are familiar enough nowadays with the determinative effects of social deprivation and privilege. Perhaps the "great leap forward" of American life in our time was the Supreme Court's decision in *Brown v. Topeka Board of Education* to outlaw the principle of "separate but equal" because enforced separation of the races is not equality. To be brought up having to recognize oneself as permanently barred from access to privileges guaranteed to one's fellows, including their company in school, is a deforming influence, although it has sometimes inspired great and successful creative effort.[6] Racial segregation is only one of the grossest cultural influences. All of us have grown up in some kind of defining tradition, and traditional structures are so much part of us that all others seem odd, even when they are enviable. However, the genetic, racial, linguistic, and social differences that are at once the matrix and the scene of our psychic life belong to another sphere of inquiry than psychoanalysis.

In narrowing the scope of our theme of becoming, we need

to reckon with family life, which psychoanalysts have made our own field of study. It is noteworthy that the psychoanalytic dialogue between patient and doctor itself recapitulates or revives family life. The doctor is variously addressed, but his presence conceals the imaginary presence of others—members of the patient's family and circle of friends in early life, now living or dead. We have reason to believe that this repetition would happen wherever early life is lived within the close social bounds of families and might be very different when upbringing is provided by professional child-carers or by tribally designated "relatives" outside the biological family. Freud's insights originated in the European family system, but I do not believe that they are limited to it if taken in their larger implications. Freud recognized that the attachments of early childhood are passionate, formative, and persistent. Humans are of absolute necessity the products of families or other social organizations that provide close, physical nurturing and active educational encouragement.[7] Humans are born helpless and only slowly become children who can more or less fend for themselves. We are much less dominated by instincts than other animals and have to be taught how to survive, to find our way through the intricate web of modern life (which might be said to have abandoned tradition in favor of bureaucracy, a yet more intricate network of involvements). But this obligatory contact with adults inside and outside the family is passionate; desires, longings, hatreds, jealousy, envy, and, above all, love—as well as equally powerful ways of concealing all of them—color our early relations.

These passionate feelings are formative, too. That is, human becoming is repetitious. What I came to feel about my mother, the special form of my attachment to her, arising from her history and our shared genetic structure and experiences, as well as from a host of relatively fortuitous events, is a part of me. I am that person who has had that mother; my brothers and sisters may have lived quite different lives with her and with our father, as well as with one another and with me.

Freud saw in these formative actions of family life a distinct pattern that he called the Oedipus complex.[x] I have often wished he hadn't given it this name, but the term is probably ineradicable and it does categorize something that exists within our nature. It is notoriously difficult to discuss this concept because of the overlay of popular misconceptions for which analysts, beginning with Freud, are partly responsible. (Only partly, because even the best expositions can be misunderstood.) The name of Oedipus, who was ineluctably ordained to kill his father and marry his mother, so enthralls the imagination that the subtlety of Freud's meaning is easily lost. Divested of mythology, the grand formulation holds that the family is the scene of passionate emotional involvements in which love and hate, centering around the members of the family, influence the later development of the individual. The signal element is rivalry, the struggle for exclusive physical and emotional possession of one or both parents. All the stratagems, ruses, and plots that we devise in our not-so-innocent childhoods to get our way— and, on the other hand, all the protective measures we take to ensure against defeat or disappointment in that campaign for possession—have the same beginnings.

It would be misleading to suggest that the Oedipus complex is the same in all histories or that it is ever enacted in full view, so to speak, of all the participants. The possible permutations of rivalry are manifold and much of the time the participants are ignorant of what is going on. Sometimes an acute external observer senses it, without any psychoanalytic prejudices. Likewise, rivalries among children are at times fully visible (and audible): witness St. Augustine's perceptive remarks about the child, already abundantly fed, who gazes balefully at its foster-sibling nursing at the breast.[9] Augustine, to be sure, shows us this picture to give empirical evidence for the doctrine of original sin: if little children can have that malevolent gaze, and presumably the hateful will that the gaze reveals, surely the disposition to sinfulness must be inborn. Some of this is obvious enough, but the heart of the matter lies in the formative influence of such sibling rivalries, or oedipal rivalries, on the development of character. By this we mean the particular ways in which we repeat our past in our encounters with the present: to win the forbidden love, to overcome the prohibitions put in our way, to be first.

The sexual difference adds another load to the burden of becoming. That humans should come in two forms is by no means self-evident to children. In fact, it appears that the initial discrimination is functional rather than anatomical: for the most part it is the mother who gives, the father being at best a secondary mother. Sometime in the early months or years of life, the child comes to know the genital difference as such. Because it is a concealed difference, the first references to it are likely to be by way of secondary sexual characteristics, or such tertiary ones as clothing. However it is that children come to observe the sex difference, it is a source of wonder and curiosity, but also of uneasiness. That something is present in one sex but absent in the other remains a mystery, which is compounded rather than solved when the distribution of authority and strength turns out to be adapted to the genital difference. All traditional expressions of the biblical religions lend supernatural power to it. It is not difficult to see that the sexual difference, like infantile helplessness and dependency, will remain a site of potential distortion throughout life.[10]

Is the child's life in the family the source only of its less desirable traits? Not as Freud saw it, and not as I see it. It is true that our recognition of the negative is profound, yet no more so than Augustine's. That there is no end to human egoism was not Freud's discovery; he has, however, anatomized it rather fully. The desire to possess, to gain control over other human beings, is so primitive as to appear innate. We may well ask whether this desire has its beginnings in the original unity of mother and child, and we may likewise wonder whether it is not the counterpart of what we think of as the fall of man. Did we lose our Paradise when we entered the world, naked and helpless and insatiable in our desire? While it seems perverse to look on our creation as itself a fall, our entrance into the family appears to recapitulate something of the sort. Our need to possess can be thought of as a need to repossess something that we lost in being born. Nevertheless, the Paradise is not quite lost; there is also a unity after birth between mother and infant. This unity is not illusory, since mothers are usually, if not always, equipped to rediscover in themselves a state of feeling corresponding to the baby's. To some extent fathers are also open to that possibility, so that the family may be, at least for a while, a scene of mutuality in which normal egoism is suspended.[11]

With or without the theological implications, the great disruption of birth is the position where most analysts start, and there is a surprising degree of unity among us on it. We have no real knowledge, as I have already noted, that life before birth, to the extent that it is in any way conscious, is one of perfect harmony. In fact, there is said to be evidence that antenatal life has anxieties of its own, evidence drawn from the analogy of fetal movements with those of infants.[12] Birth is attended by the great separation that institutes the powerful demands which issue in our desires, and the becoming of a person may be thought of as a history of desire. To return to Augustine, "our hearts are restless." Our desires never repose completely, but it is from outside psychoanalysis that we draw the rest of Augustine's figure: "until they rest in Thee."[13]

To accomplish our desires, we need to love and be loved. It is really quite remarkable that it should be so, commonplace as the words sound. Many people's recollections of early life in the family are so fraught with misery that their response to such a contention can only be cynical. I have always had a sneaking admiration, along with some pity, for the novelist Samuel Butler's rueful comment that it would have been better if humans were born like certain moths, after the death of their parents, but wrapped up in five-pound notes! Butler gave due recognition to the horrors of a particular sort of Victorian Anglican upbringing, so vividly narrated in his *Way of All Flesh*, and it is quite true that every life we have the opportunity of analyzing is marked by the sense of the deficiencies of parents and siblings. That is clearly not the whole story. Far from being born posthumously, like the moth, we are from our beginning surrounded by adults, preferably parents who instinctively treasure their offspring beyond all else in their lives and thereby create a certain contagion of love. It is an intensely physical love—one wants to say "incarnate", of the flesh—not only in feeding and giving drink, but in holding, caressing, soothing, dressing and undressing, making agreeable noises, presenting interesting objects. Without some physical expressions of love, the child just doesn't "become"; it languishes and dies. Even an impoverished expression of love is better than none.

We cannot know whether other animals also feel this way about their young, but to think otherwise, of mammals at least, seems monstrous. Barry Lopez, in his marvelous book *Arctic Dreams*, recounts the story of a polar bear mother forced by bored and sadistic sailors to witness the pointless killing of her cubs. Her evident lamentation and pain recalls to the reader's mind the slaughter of other innocents.[14] Like many matters in the evolution of man's mind, I find the evidence that precursors of human love are present in animals more persuasive of its divine origin than the contrary. It ought to have a bearing on our religious and ethical life that the foundations of our existence—physical, emotional, moral, mental—lie in the caring of strong adults for weak infants, and, equally important, that the memory of this absolute dependency is the ground on which all later relations are figured.

It is necessary to consider that our lives fall into epochs that slowly dawn (after the literally precipitate event of our birth), advance, reach a peak, then recede and merge with the next. Man is a temporal creature in other ways, too. We know how different the sense of time is in early childhood and later in life. We can recollect the interminable quality of time in some periods of early life, especially in contrast with the evanescence of days in old age. It helps to understand the power of early experience if we look at it in its temporal dimension. The events of childhood carry their immense impact partly because they had to be lived with over what seemed to be aeons, rather than as fleeting elements in the passage of time. A death close to the child is sometimes barely noticed, to all external appearances, but it is worked over and over in innumerable contexts in that period of slow time and becomes woven into the fabric of the child's character. Events of lesser magnitude are sometimes exaggerated quite out of proportion (from the adult point of view) because they hurt the child on a certain day and were slowly fitted into contexts that perpetuated the anguish. I recall a young man's unabated misery at the memory of having been teased as a little boy for his squeamishness over baiting a fishhook with a worm. Such simple events, from the seeming triviality of the young man's misery to the catastrophic disaster of the death of a loved one, give direction and focus to the life of the little person, for whom they exist in another temporal mode than the adult's.

I would like to stress another point in talking about becoming: its variability. It should be plain that, granted the manifold circumstances of human life, inner experience must vary widely. Our genetic inheritance, early experiences, and so forth are never alike, however similar they may be statistically. Each of us has grasped his existence differently from the beginning. Analysts have the difficult task of simultaneously holding in their minds personal variations and the great similitudes and correspondences of life, which Heinz Hartmann called "the average expectable environment";[15] that is, to see not only the usual experiences of different times and places, but also the unique application of these catagories in every individual life. These uniquenesses have always been the most interesting part of psychoanalysis. I think it was St. Thomas Aquinas who wrote that every angel is itself a species; while I am not quite prepared to say that every human is a species, that is mainly because Thomas and we moderns probably use the word differently.

So when we say that this or that "behavior" characterizes

the person at a given age, we may be right, but we also show the limitations of the word *behavior.* One teenager's aloofness conceals extreme shyness or shame about sexual maturation; another's marks resentment of adult demands; and still another's is the outward presentation of a richly imaginative life. All these and many other experiences come and go in the one adolescent period.

When we speak of stages, periods, or epochs of life, we allude to the reality that humans, considered as subjective beings, always face the future, however much their lives are influenced by the past. Analysts are so concerned to know about the past, to understand how what happened then is effective now, that we sometimes pay too little attention to our patients' concern for what is to come. Yet we talk a lot about desire, the motor influence of all life, which is always oriented to the future.[16] Even when patients indulge the futile wish to change their past by saying such things as "If only I'd had parents as understanding as you" (ignoring that the analyst's children might think otherwise), they are usually expressing the intention of making something better happen in the future. The person who simply "lives just for the present" is one whose grasp of the future is short; he still makes plans and has intentions for today and tomorrow, if not for next year. Most of us extend our intentions even into the remote future, partly because we accept responsibility for the fate of those entrusted to us, partly out of more immediate self-interest. Such concerns for the future may be a serious liability, too: a wide spectrum of concern exists covering happy anticipation, serious planning, perpetual worry, or obsessional paralysis. All have in common the acknowledgment of an unknown future. But there is good reason to believe that our disposition to one or another of these attitudes or states is grounded in our past.

Expectations must change as we get older. I have heard that Freud, who was not given to piety, was asked what could benefit the aging single woman whom psychoanalysis has belatedly freed from the restrictions that have hitherto kept her from love and marriage. "Something has to be left to 'der liebe Gott'," he replied. Possibilities change with advancing age; recognizing this as both a limitation and an extension of our existence is one of the mixed benefits of what we call "maturing." I am the same person that I was at age twelve, twenty-four, or forty, but I am also different. This enduring wonder confronts the analyst as he tries to understand what the patient felt during different epochs of life and what bearing those feelings have on the present and future.

The red thread running through our analytic study of change and becoming is the thread of desire. What we look for in analyzing a patient is an answer, or perhaps some of the many answers, to the question "What do you want?" We may claim that this is an unnecessary question, that we know what we want but just don't know how to get it. This is also a truth. But the psychoanalytic fact of the matter is that more often than not it is indeed not knowing what we want that causes the confusion of our lives, because what we want is in great measure hidden from us. That is why psychoanalysis was invented, so to speak: to help reveal unrecognized desires.

The most uniquely human knowledge we have is that at some time we will have no future at all, will not "become" anything any more, will be spoken of only in the past tense. We face death as the end of our becoming, of our intentions, of our desires. I believe that Miguel de Unamuno was right in stating quite flatly that such a prospect is intolerable to us, for all our brave denial of the fear of death, and indeed of death itself, as if it were something that happened only to other people.[7] But I shall save further reflections on this matter for our consideration of "ending" in chapter 7.

Notes

1. According to N. Chomsky, humans have a predisposition to grammatical language. This "universal grammar" is the innate structure for language, although it requires the experience of language in the environment

to make it work. See Chomsky's *Knowledge of Language: Its Nature, Origin and Use* (New York: Praeger, 1986).

2. See Jean Itard, "The Wild Boy of Aveyron" in Lucien Malson, ed., *Wolf Children and the Problem of Human Nature* (New York: Monthly Review Press, 1971). For all its interest and pathos, the story of the "wild boy" may be misleading. Itard, who devoted five years of his life to the child known as Victor, claimed that he was merely a normal child subjected to a feral upbringing. Most authorities, however, prefer the diagnosis of feeblemindedness.

3. "The child bathes in language," wrote H. Delacroix in *Le Langage et la pensée* (quoted by M. Merleau-Ponty in *Consciousness and the Acquisition of Language*, trans. H. J. Silverman [Evanston: Northwestern University Press, 1973], p. 12). Merleau-Ponty's essay is a philosophical summary of work on the development of language before 1950. It is a rich phenomenological account. While the psycholinguistic picture has altered since Merleau-Ponty's time (as the above reference to N. Chomsky attests), the situation of the child in the speaking world remains the same.

4. Among psychoanalysts, the foremost exponent of this view is Jacques Lacan, whose influence will be evident throughout these pages. A first approximation of his theory is in his "Mirror Stage as Formative of the I" and "The Function and Field of Speech and Language in Psychoanalysis," in *Ecrits*, trans. Alan Sheridan (New York: W. W. Norton, 1977). The tie of the image to the object submits to the more fluid dominance of language, whereby the experience of the external world acquires meanings. The shifting significations of words provide all-important nuances of speech, through which the uniquenesses of individuals are mediated. But the one-to-one presymbolic identity of the visual image with the physical object persists, especially in our dreamlife.

5. The question of genetic origins of mental qualities has always been a troublesome one for psychoanalysts and others. Freud proposed that inborn dispositions determined the development of the desires ("instincts," in his language). Psychoanalysts have preferred not to make much of the foundation of all experience in the inherited structure, emphasizing instead the determining influences of events in the history of the person. Obviously, it is the effect of these events that is open to change; but to ignore genetic origins often means to define the "normal" too narrowly and to have unwarranted expectations of both parents and offspring.

6. For a highly personal discussion, see R. Coles, *Children of Crisis* (Boston: Little, Brown, 1967).

7. Many years ago, R. Spitz had the opportunity of testing this hypothesis in a humane fashion by contrasting the relative flourishing of babies living in a women's prison, where they could be tended by their mothers, with the decline of babies in a poorly-staffed institution where the over-

worked nurses had no time to provide more than the basic necessities. Spitz's article, entitled "Hospitalism: An Enquiry into the Genesis of Psychiatric Conditions in Early Childhood," was published in the annual *Psychoanalytic Study of the Child* 1 (1945).

8. I have written about the Oedipus complex as a hermeneutic myth in "Demythologizing Oedipus," *The Psychoanalytic Quarterly* 54, no. 3 (1985). In some ways, the process of "demythologizing"—that is, of separating the experiences that constitute the term *Oedipus complex* from the myth in which it is embedded—has been the task of psychoanalysis ever since Freud applied the name.

9. "I myself have seen and observed a jealous baby: it didn't yet speak, but it gazed wanly and with a bitter look at its fellow nurseling" (Augustine *Confessions* 1.7).

10. As well as being a pioneer, Freud was a man of his times. He showed this clearly in his understanding of the sex difference and in his attitude to religion. There is a curious symmetry between Freud's stated suppositions about the subordinate role of women and those embedded in Judeo-Christian tradition. Consequently, he and his followers have been accused of a conservatism with respect to femininity that sits oddly with the more usual accusation of subversion. A careful reading of Freud's writings on sexuality, at least with hindsight, permits us to distinguish to some extent between the observations he made about the human grasp of the sex difference and the cultural values superimposed on it. That male dominance has been closely tied to the visibly impressive male genital is as close to positive knowledge as we can have in a field where we depend on subjective reports. That this connection has been exploited to extend or maintain male dominance is an inference that was far less easily drawn a half century ago than now. Far from promoting male dominance (allegedly through the theory of "penis-envy"), psychoanalysis has undermined it by another subversion: it has shown that the genital basis of male superiority is an illusion, created more by male anxiety than by female longing. Freud's writings on sexuality, especially female sexuality, are well known. A useful, if not entirely lucid, reinterpretation is J. Lacan's "Signification of the Phallus," in *Ecrits* (see n. 5 above). In Lacan's view, the male organ in its vivid externality becomes the signifier of values, including the sacred, that are the actual reasons for the assumption of male superiority.

11. Among classical psychoanalysts, Hans Loewald has brought out this aspect of early life with special clarity. He has suggested its importance for our later, "mature" grasp of reality, in contrast to some other analysts, who regard the mother-child "matrix" exclusively as a stage to be superseded in the interest of an "objective" point of view. Loewald has examined this matter from many sides; I specially recommend the articles "Ego and Real-

ity" (1949) and "On Motivation and Instinct Theory" (1971), both in *Papers on Psychoanalysis* (New Haven: Yale University Press, 1980).

12. P. Greenacre summarized the studies made before 1941 of the seemingly "anxious" movements of the fetus in "The Predisposition to Anxiety," *Psychoanalytic Quarterly* 10, nos. 1 and 4 (1941).

13. *Confessions* 1.1.

14. Barry Lopez, *Arctic Dreams* (New York: Scribner's, 1986), p. 112.

15. Also "the typical average environment." See Heinz Hartmann, "Psychoanalysis and the Concept of Health," *International Journal of Psychoanalysis* 20 (1939), p. 319.

16. On the interrelationships of past, present, and future in psychoanalysis, see H. W. Loewald, "Superego and Time" (1962) and "The Experience of Time" (1971), in *Papers on Psychoanalysis*.

17. Miguel de Unamuno, *The Tragic Sense of Life*, trans. J. E. Crawford Flitch (New York: Dover, 1954), especially pp. 38–57. This work by the Basque philosopher is an outcry against death on behalf of eternal life. It appeared in Spanish in 1913 and in English in 1921, but the main issue— the timeless struggle of faith and skepticism—remains fresh. The usual arguments against immortality are faced openly and honestly, not least the psychoanalytic "wish-fulfillment."

· 3 ·

Loving and Hating

The family as the initial setting of our life is by the same token the primary source of our loves and hates. We have already taken this up in relation to the Oedipus complex and sibling rivalry, more or less as formulas for the interrelationships within the family, with all the complexities of loving and hating present from the beginnings of life. I have also referred to our mammalian inheritance of caring for the young, especially maternal caring, as one of the prerequisites of our existence. The mother, or whoever takes her place, is the absolute center and source of all good—but also of all refusal of good. The inevitable refusal of good initiates the experience of badness. It is only educated conjecture that helps us sort out these literally very primitive feelings of fulfillment of desire and unfulfillment of desire, feelings that have not yet become verbalized thoughts. We believe that they are nevertheless present as images of some kind in the infant's mind, playing an active part in motivation and in the laying down of a character structure. As the source of satisfaction of basic physiological needs, a mother exists for the child as identical with the stuff she gives and with the child's good feelings. At this stage of life, there is no distinct difference between inside and outside.

But if the giver of pleasure is by that fact good, then the withholder of pleasure is bad, in the only sense that "bad" can have in early infancy—not an ethical sense, but a state of feeling. It is perhaps a combination of the feeling of unabated hunger and inner emptiness with rage, another innate response. Connecting that boiling over of rage in its piercingly unpleasant quality with the need for food has been developed in human evolution as a life-saving device, if only on account of the sheer annoyance or the guilt about negligence that it can induce in the parents. As a subjective state, it is the forerunner of hating. So, too, this feeling that corresponds to deprivation and emptiness is not referred to a separated inside and outside. Mother as nongiver is hated and is also felt as the source of that hatred, along with the unpleasant emptiness.[1]

Whoever or whatever seems to stand in the way of gratification—or, like the father some of the time, is just an indifferent third party—is likely to come to represent the refusal of good. He or she puts limits to satisfaction merely by existing and absorbing some of the giver's time, while being in part a giver, too. This double split in the roles of the mother and father, either of whom can be the good or the bad parent, probably supports the structure of what later in life becomes the foundation for our emotional appreciation of the larger world.

The evident point of this picture is that our lives are locked in struggle and in conflict of feelings from the outset; our first loves are also our first hates. Although it is unquestionably desirable for love to predominate, it is inevitable for it to be countered by its opposite in some important respects. That is why it is hopelessly artificial to try to deal with these emotions separately. This observation is not unfamiliar to parents or to those who have observed children closely in other ways. The view of children as sweet innocents living in a purely happy world has departed, if indeed it ever prevailed outside very sentimental hearts.

The course of true love being rough even in childhood, it is not surprising that it remains so later in life. By a wordless axiom, whoever or whatever is "good" and loved is supposed to be reliably and selflessly gratifying in perpetuity. The bad feelings that fulminate in us when we are deprived are attributed to the person whom we love and from whom we expect love—and only love. One might say without too much exaggeration that all human sorrow, as well as intolerance and often violence, come from disappointment in love. The personification of an external disaster or natural danger may have played a large part in the formation of beliefs in gods and other supernatural forces, and I am persuaded that the roots of such beliefs include blaming our parents for their failure to maintain us. William James wrote of something like this after he felt the shocks of an earthquake in California. That it had been jokingly predicted to him by a friend in Massachusetts made the personification readier, but James affirmed that "animus and intent were never more present in any human action." It was, after all, our mother, the Earth, that had betrayed him.[2]

For all that, selfless love not only exists but is essential to our being human. It needs examination, too. It isn't "selfless" at all, if by that we mean a kind of devotion to another that is unaccompanied by any feeling of pleasure, satisfaction, approval, or just care, all of which are rewarding in themselves. The deep identity of oneself with another, deriving from the early identity of mother and child, here delivers a powerful ethical potential: I cannot do good to anyone else without having a sense of inner good, as well. This is "at heart" not self-praise or pride in my own virtue, but a sense of being that other person myself. In a quite literal sense, when we love our neighbor we also love ourselves. Even little children from time to time show genuine altruism in their conduct, although it is hardly fair to expect it of them (or of anyone else, for that matter). Still, it is worth marveling that even a person who often appears wrapped up in himself or herself is human to the extent that he or she can imagine and thereby share the subjective state of another. At such times we can know what another person is thinking, put ourselves in his or her shoes, as we say. The very fact of language presupposes such a state of affairs, for when we speak we plunge into a communion with our fellow speakers. Loving others is by nature a communion with their inner world.

What, then, is love? So far it seems to be an emotion that finds its expression in attachment, liking, and caring. We are bidden to love our neighbor as ourselves. The illustration given us by Jesus—if it is permissible to translate the biblical parable from a sociological perspective—is one of concerned attendance by a foreigner on a distressed, neglected member of the dominant community. That is, Christian love, charity, or agape is a form of principled action, not an emotion at all. In the one brief but memorable conversation I had with W. H. Auden, the poet struck vigorously against the notion that the Samaritan need have in the least liked the man who had fallen among thieves and whom he befriended. I held, and hold, that even when loving action springs from principle and no feeling of love or liking can be among its motives, such feelings must nevertheless enter in for the action to be more than a gesture. Unless we are only bureaucratic administrators, our prompting to loving action needs to come from that sense of oneness with the object of charity that finds its beginnings in the unity of mother (or parent) and child. I am constantly struck by the psychological profundity of the Christian injunction to love as its central commandment; as the modern Christian martyr Dietrich Bonhoeffer repeatedly reminded us, such love means "being-for-others," a state on which human existence depends from the beginning to the end. The point of Jesus' great second commandment is that it takes into account the variability of loving as a human emotion and summons us to loving action, however limited our emotional equipment may be. Yet, as I have also commented, loving is by no means an automatic or universal state of mind.

Some limits must be put on our panegyric of love. We cannot fathom its mysteries or extol its benefits enough. All that Paul has said on the subject in his first letter to the Corinthians is psychologically true. But the praise of love becomes a burden sometimes, and not a useful one. We have to understand that we differ in the capacity for loving others and in the quality of our love. Whether these differences are God-given, inborn, or due to accidents of development is not so much to the point as knowing that they exist. Without some forbearance, we are apt to injure others by making unjust judgments: some people are not especially loving by nature and yet have their own contributions to make in other ways. Psychoanalysts sometimes propose inverse proportions between love and self-love: if a person does not become attached to others, then love of self must have preempted the field. I hope to give that thought due consideration when I come to discuss disorder in human life, but here I want only to offer a caution against the not-very-hidden invidious moral judgment implicit in such formulas. Detached or unattached people are not at all necessarily in love with themselves. Loving, beyond an irreducible minimum, is a talent not universally shared. Along with other virtuous states, it has a history in the individual that prepares him or her to love, fail to love, or resist love under new conditions of life. There is much to be said for the Christian principles that we do not earn our way to salvation by virtuous works and that God's love is ahead of ours.

As I remarked at the beginning of this chapter, love and hate seem to have common origins; that is, the same persons—usually parents—are the objects of both feelings, because gratification and deprivation, pleasure and unpleasure, come from them. It is from this division within the child's affections, from loving and hating the same person, that the sense of *guilt* arises. Through this agency, the loving self punishes the bad self. This process is very intricate and therefore controversial, but I have always thought it evidence of the moral depth of psychoanalysis that it attempts to understand such a remarkable and uniquely human characteristic.[3] The simplest statement of it that I know is that the loved one, who is the good one, comes to be the good part of oneself and in this way makes inner condemnation take the place of parental condemnation. Disobedience, our first sin in the biblical myth, is inevitable because our desire as infants does not always correspond to what is offered us by loving parents. We may literally bite the hand or the breast that feeds us; there is a powerful wisdom in the story that mankind's first offense was eating forbidden fruit. Augustine eloquently tells the tale in the *Confessions* of stealing pears with the other boys of his little gang, not because they were hungry or wanted to sell the pears, but just because it was wrong.[4] And is not disobedience an act of hate against the one we love and who loves us?

The intimate connection between guilt and sin has earned the pondering of Christians over millennia. It is not likely to be solved by psychological considerations, but we have learned that the capacity to feel guilt is what assures us of our recognition of sin, and also, to my mind, that sin is "about" failure to love. This is a far cry from the traditional popular attitudes, rejected by Jesus, that sin is mainly an infraction of social or moral rules. To be sure, such infractions may themselves be acts of disobedience to God or of hostility to our neighbor, but they may only express opposition to socially hallowed habits that do not differ ethically from others long discarded.

As a psychoanalyst I can hardly leave the question of love at that. Nor should anyone. It is all very well to speak deprecatingly of the debasement of the word *love* in popular use, which narrows its meaning to romantic or sexual love. Certain Christian tendencies have perhaps played their part in this alleged debasement by making radical disjunctions between carnal and spiritual love. It will not do here to go on about Gnostic and Manichaean influences; I suspect that modern Christians like to fob off on the heretics some of the perplexities that orthodoxy has got us into. Indeed, preoccupation with virginity and chastity has been characteristic of Christianity since its early years, making sexlessness an attribute of perfection for the orthodox quite as much as for the heretics. On the other hand, normative Christianity and Judaism have had the wisdom to glorify marriage while assuming that their adherents would not "live like angels."[5] The psychoanalytic interpretation of the love-life asserts rather that the two meanings of love—ultimate concern for others and passionate desire for sexual union with a precious other—have common as well as diverse origins in human life. Thus, it is wrong to ignore either.

Psychoanalysis theorizes that love as concern for others is a later, rather disembodied form of what begins as physical passion. I have never liked the term *sublimation*, which in physical science means a transformation from the solid to the gaseous state. In psychoanalytic usage, it depends on a theory of love that is based on an ambivalent view of sexuality: sublimation is good because it permits higher culture to take place as energies are redirected from the passions to the creative and spiritual, but it is bad because it may deplete the resources and leave nothing for bodily satisfaction. Freud may have shown his misgivings in his amusing analogy of sublimation with the frugal peasant who saved his pennies by giving his ox one straw of hay less every day; all went very well for a while, but the poor animal eventually starved to death. In its way, this amusing anecdote is a cautionary reminder that culture or even religion is not a substitute for bodily satisfaction. It is misleading, however, in its implied reciprocal. Like its Christian parallel, the psychoanalytic axiom says: "The more passion, the less charity." I don't think that claim bears close examination. Chastity and charity, or chastity and cultural achievement, are not causally related. It should be added that the theory of sublimation is usually so stated as to involve quite other matters than adult genital sexuality; more primitive desires, it is claimed, find their way into the "higher" spheres.

Sexuality, the power that generates all life, has always occupied a central place in psychoanalytic thought. Freud's very name has become synonymous with sexuality and would have even if it did not itself mean "joy." Coming into being in the heyday of Victorian prudery, with its vast sexual underworld, psychoanalysis shocked the world by speaking plainly of forbidden topics and, worse still, by insisting on the importance of the sexual life in health and disorder.[6] The original discoveries of the power of sexual restrictions, repressions, inhibitions, and taboos in providing the groundwork for neurotic disorders, proved formative in Freud's construction of his whole theory of man's inner life. The term *sexual* was extended into all the realms of desire, from infancy to old age and running the gamut of human concern. Although this proliferation has given rise to misunderstanding, I give it still a pretty ungrudging admiration: to the world that pretended, and sometimes still pretends, that sexuality doesn't exist if you don't notice it, Freudian language countered that it was omnipresent, and even omnipotent, except when opposed by hatred and death. Later theory has if anything underplayed sexuality or transferred it to the elusive concept of "instinct," which is supposed to link psychoanalysis to biology, although the term *instinct*, as psychoanalysts use it, is biologically unrecognizable.

To place sexuality in the psychoanalytical image of man, we need to think about desire, a subjective state that is rooted in our physical nature and expressed through our bodies, but becomes through our experience something far more complex than a blind physical urge. Like loving in its more general sense, sexual desire is not uniformly distributed. There are those in whom it is only slightly present, and, of course, fluctuations in intensity of desire are universal. Why is it that in many religions, not only Christianity, the absence of sexual desire is so highly prized? Particularly in women, naturally, since the dominant male sex has always liked to pretend that its disposition to promiscuity was the work of the tempting female. It is convenient—and at times probably true—to believe that celibacy, which has proven value in some religious communities, is more practical in the absence of desire. But in the main we can see that sexuality is problematic to religion whether it welcomes celibacy or not. Thus, desire tends to be looked down on. It was no wonder that the churchmen who established the canon of our Bible (in evident imitation of the Jewish scholars before them) were at pains to instruct readers of the Song of Songs, the most gloriously erotic of all ancient writings, that it represented not the joys of human sexual love, but the love of Christ and the church.[7]

One explanation for religious antisexual prejudice can be confirmed by psychoanalytic experience, although it was not discovered by psychoanalysis: sexuality is possessive. The disposition to jealousy begins early and the possibility of infidelity arouses the deepest ire in the young child. This is the basis for the sexual jealousy of adults. The *crime passionel* is not even punished in some parts of the world, recognizing as people do the lengths to which sexual jealousy will go. Of course, we don't explain fidelity and the injunction against adultery by reference to jealousy alone: there are high values of commitment and caring in monogamy and the lasting family that deserve protection. But the suffering caused by sexual disappointment is very great. Again, we can see in this the identification of the object of one's love with important parts of ourselves: to be threatened with loss of love is to be threatened with loss of self. Sexuality only reinforces this with its bodily energies.

We have also learned more in psychoanalysis about how easily sexuality lapses into being considered a degraded state through its physical association with the excretory organs. Just as the socialization of children requires them to control and segregate their excretory functions, so cultural advance seems to demand control and segregation of the sexual function. The quality of "purity" is akin to that of cleanliness, the result being that men and women are apt to be apologetic about their sexuality, as if it were a socially objectionable function that needed special justification, preferably by clergy.

The evolutionary connection between sexuality and procreation does not itself play any manifest role in man's psychic life; that is, procreation is in our consciousness only as a secondary, derived end of sexual relations. At the deepest levels we discover the persistent desire to recreate the nuclear family, to be the father or mother that we once had, with the expectable corollary in our firm intention to do the job better. At least this is so among people raised in European and American societies. One hears so often in the conscious or unconscious expressions of patients, comparisons between their own upbringing and what they would or do design for their children. Sometimes such resolutions are successful and one feels that progress is being made, at least for one generation, but they may also institute reactions that are equally hard for the young to endure—overpermissiveness in substitution for overcontrol, for example.

Only lately has the world (or a small part of it) reluctantly become willing to see that sexual desire may have nothing at all to do with procreation. I refer to homosexuality, while regretting the word, since giving a "scientific" name to love and desire within one's own sex extends to it a clinical presumption. Freud made the revolutionary discovery that beneath the surface of conscious sexual desire for the opposite sex lies a "counterwill" in the form of desire for one's own sex. People feel in the unconscious desire for the same sex something of the nature of an internal threat; the frank presence of such a desire in others offers an external threat that needs to be suppressed in the interest of self-protection. Freud went far beyond this discovery and inferred that conscious homosexual love was itself due to some defect in the development of "normal" love. Despite "gay liberation," most of the world still operates on that principle, because the splitting between conscious and unconscious desire is universal and social change is only a partial answer. It has not yet become common opinion that the capacity for homosexual love is an extension rather than a restriction of loving. Here, too, the ancient call to hatred is readily awakened: whatever feels bad inside is linked to a bad source outside. It is remarkable how often the most severe condemnation of a disliked character, and the one he is most likely to deny, is directed against his supposed or actual deviation from the accepted sexual norm. While psychoanalysis has enlightened us in respect to the universality of homosexual strivings and feelings, it has harmed many homosexual people by convincing them, as well as their society, that their strongest impulses and greatest pleasures are symptoms of disorder.[8]

I hope that I have not departed too far from the "image of God" in this discussion. For me, loving and hating are the most revealing of all human capacities to resemble God as he has been revealed to us, and to depart from that resemblance. God, we say, hates nothing that he has made and so loved the world that he entered as a human into human fate and history. He also showed his love in our capacity for love, including sexual love, as John Milton wrote.[9] Our minds and bodies are at one in the possibility of attachment, caring, protection, giving. Human fulfillment is never adequate when it is only fulfillment of the self: the other who cares, or the others who care, are the guarantors of our personal fulfillment. Humans need to love and be loved, although, as I have found it essential to remember, no one can precisely define for anyone else just what kind of love that ought to be.

The other side of the story is not far to seek. We fail at every point to live out that God-like claim on us. All manner of experience turns us away from it. Self-love is built into us as much as loving. Love and self-love arise from the same stock: is not my self-love ultimately dependent on the love my parents showed me? They nevertheless diverge, again because of the disappointments that we undergo in our expectations of others. Our love is contingent: I love you only if you love me. This is no longer the *imago dei*.

Since Freud, psychoanalysts have made much of self-love, in ways that are supposed to be neutral but often are not. Once again, as with Oedipus, we have been made captive by a name, that of Narcissus. Freud found it convenient to link together a very long series of human conditions in which he saw the common factor of self-concern, and he named them in honor of that mythical figure whose lot it was to fall in love with his own reflection. Such preoccupation with one's own appearance is frequent enough, although not often as exclusive as in Narcissus' case, but the spread of the idea of narcissism to cover every kind of concern about oneself, including one's internal organs, or extensions of oneself like one's work or one's children has in the long run clouded matters rather than illuminated them. Not that any of such preoccupations is unreal; far from it. But to assume that they have special underlying connections seems to me merely a case of infatuation with Narcissus.

Self-hate is no less a human problem than self-love, and it offers great opportunity for confusion of meaning. Take, for example, any of the general confessions in the liturgy. An outsider coming unprepared into a church during the recitation of a confession or of the litany might well shake his head pityingly at the abject lack of self-esteem of the members of this congregation. How they berate themselves, especially in the confession with the words "spare us miserable offenders" and "there is no health in us," but even in the alternative one containing the phrase "the burden of them is intolerable." How they must hate themselves! And what a surprise to see a bit later that most of these penitents, far from wearing hair shirts, look pretty cheerful, sometimes even joyous, and after Mass reward themselves with sherry and cakes. That is an example of the dangers of mere behaviorism in human psychology. Although the penitents who say those or similar confessions are seriously lamenting their sins, they are also confident of forgiveness. To suggest, as someone might thoughtlessly do by an abuse of psychoanalytic principles, that such penitents, however cheerful in appearance, are unconsciously guiltier than nonbelievers who never make confessions betrays psychoanalytical ignorance. In their confessions, penitents do not hate themselves in the way of depressives, unless they happen to be depressed, too. Christian self-hatred is real enough, arising, like all self-judgment, from the contrasting vision of what we are and what we are called on to be. But—and here is the literal crux of the matter—we know all the while that for God the best we can do is enough, since he has already forgiven our sins. It is refreshing to read the words from the *Didache* or *Teachings of the Twelve Apostles*, dating from the second century or earlier: "If you can bear the whole yoke of the Lord, you will be perfect, but if you can't, do what you can."[10] That little advice, if we can take it without self-exculpation or smugness, might be a useful remedy against self-hatred of the wrong kind. It should be unnecessary to add that Jews derive a like benefit from the exposure of their souls to a forgiving "father and king" in the penitential prayers of Yom Kippur.

I have purposely brought these similar ideas together—Christian self-hatred and psychoanalytic narcissism—because the effort may help us to distinguish the different meanings among seemingly related terms. In addition, they point to an idea implicit in both Christianity and psychoanalysis: that love for others is preferable to love for oneself, of whatever kind.

Serious questions about hating are left unanswered by psychoanalytic understanding. I have never treated a thoroughgoing hater, of the kind not to be confused with the rest of us ordinary beings who may be irascible, vindictive, or mischievous from time to time, or show other such unlovely qualities when we are (or fancy that we are) mistreated. While rarely commented on, the fact is that it takes a genuine desire to please to bring one to more than a passing encounter with analysis or analysts. Sometimes the desire to please serves as an obstacle to the treatment, but its absence, and the contrary dominance of an overall ragefulness and destructiveness in a person's character, seems to rule out the possibility of this kind of treatment. Patients with a low capacity for guilt-feeling are the closest to the haters that have been studied, and with them the therapeutic hope is that they will discover that guilt, unpleasant as it is, is better than the desert they have created for themselves by alienating everyone.[11] Most of our patients are all too capable of guilt. But the real hater, who would like to hurt and destroy his fellows, individually or en masse, is too well protected from guilt to seek help for his unhappiness. It is a mistake to look on this kind of hatred as sadism writ large, as if all of us were potential mass-murderers or torturers. Anyone may indulge at times in sadistic fantasies. The roots of evil are universal, but the reasons for enactment of it can at best only be guessed at by psychoanalysts. The mind of an Adolf Eichmann or a Klaus Barbie may be called "banal," but it must have been very different from the banal minds of many other diligent administrators.[12] To be able without guilt to pride oneself on the efficiency of one's technique of annihilating one's harmless and helpless fellows, whether it be one or a million, as if they were noxious insects or viruses, requires a highly specialized trait, not just a gross magnification of normal nastiness.

Such hatred I consider to be radical evil. By it the basic communion that exists between human beings has been vitiated. We analysts cannot say what events of early life, if any, predispose to radical evil, because we have no accounts of them to turn to, no "stories." Nor can we liken radical evil to the ordinary although horrible evil of war, the human instruments of which, however deceived, are usually performing what they conceive to be their duty, in self-defense and without hatred. We have learned from the analysis of soldiers and ex-soldiers that they share the common lot, although opportunities are always provided by war to bring out the worst as well as the best in human nature.

Some thinkers in psychoanalysis hold that the disposition to destructiveness is universal and primary; that it requires no disappointments, losses, or betrayals to make itself known.[13] I have pondered much on this and have not been convinced, if only because we do not have instances, or histories, of lives not subjected from birth to loss, disappointment, and so on. Maybe for this reason I have recourse to a quite unpsychological explanation (if we can call it that) for radical evil: the absolute reverse of eros, which is divine, is the diabolical.

Notes

1. The assumption that the child's inner world is composed in this fashion—that is, by mentally appropriating parts of the parents as they are

experienced and extruding hateful inner parts into the persons outside—is a theory that can, of course, be attested to only by inferences. These are drawn mainly from the play-analysis of children and the study of psychotics, who sometimes show in their actions and language aspects of thought that are not accessible in other people. The theory has been most fully developed by Melanie Klein and her followers. A less dramatic but perhaps subtler understanding is that of Hans Loewald, for whom the "mother-child" matrix is the basic unit out of which the child's world grows. See "The Psychogenesis of Manic-Depressive States" (1934) in Klein's *Contributions to Psychoanalysis, 1921–45* (London: Hogarth Press, 1948) and "On Internalization" (1973) in Loewald's *Papers on Psychoanalysis* (New Haven: Yale University Press, 1980).

2. William James, *Memories and Studies* (New York: Longmans, Green, 1911), p. 212ff. This incident is quoted and remarked on at length by Henri Bergson in *Two Sources of Morality and Religion*, trans. R. Ashley Audra, Cloudesley Brereton, and W. Horsfall Carter (New York: Holt, 1935). Both James and Bergson take up this inclination to personalize events without referring to its possible origins in infantile illusions about omnipotent parents, who also support the omnipotence of infantile wishes. But the disposition to attribute such literally shocking events as an earthquake to a being who has conscious intent seems to derive from primitive sources. Bergson even asserts that while such experiences are known as "malicious and perhaps wicked," they are also drawn to us "with something sociable and human about them" by being individualized and personalized.

3. Just how early in life a sense of guilt begins is by no sense fully understood. More important than knowing whether it depends on the child's identification with a parent at an earlier or a later age is the recognition achieved by psychoanalysis that guilt feeling requires not only the fear but also the love of an internalized parent. It will be plain to the reader who is familiar with the usual language of psychoanalysis that by avoiding technical terminology I have lost important nuances in the argument. See H. W. Loewald, "Internalization, Separation, Mourning, and the Superego," in *Papers on Psychoanalysis*, and R. Schafer, "The Loving and Beloved Superego," in *Psychoanalytic Study of the Child* (New York: International Universities Press, 1960), vol. 15.

4. *Confessions* 2.4.

5. "Living like Angels" is the title of a chapter of *Pagans and Christians* by Robin Lane Fox (New York: Alfred A. Knopf, 1987). Fox, drawing from a wide range of examples, portrays the anxious efforts of official Christianity in the second to the fourth centuries to derogate sexuality and promote virginity. He also accounts for the growing acceptance that Christians would not become "virtuous" by angelic standards. Fox opposes the view that

paganism was sexually lawless, although he recognizes that its morality was far less threatening than that of Judaism and Christianity.

6. Our principal authority on Victorian sexuality, Peter Gay, has sharply and cogently criticized the traditional picture. While Victorian propriety maintained silence about sexual life in the interest of its avowed ideal of purity, Gay shows that the personal lives of nineteenth-century men and women reveal an enthusiasm for erotic experience that would do credit to our outspoken generation. In point of fact, if we can generalize from the accounts cited by Gay, Victorians appear to have enjoyed their sexual lives with far less inner conflict than our published moderns; see *The Bourgeois Experience*, vol. 1 (New York: Oxford University Press, 1984). Steven Marcus, in *The Other Victorians* (New York: Basic Books, 1966), suggests a contrary view.

7. Even bearing in mind the preference for asceticism of early Christianity and its influence throughout the centuries as a sort of ideal, it is noteworthy that so few Christian thinkers have held for the contrary ideal: that sexual desire and sexual pleasure, at least within marriage, may well stand for the divine love. It is not as if equally radical persuasions outside the realm of sexuality have been so muted. Among modern thinkers there has been one outstanding representative of this point of view, Vladimir Soloviev, the Russian Orthodox mystical philosopher of the late nineteenth and early twentieth centuries. In his book *The Meaning of Love* (1892–94) and elsewhere, Soloviev boldly proclaimed the correspondence of sexual love to God's love and the likeness of sexual union to union with God: "In sexual love, truly understood and truly realized, this Divine essence receives the means for its definitive, ultimate incarnation in the individual life of a human, the means of the most profound and at the same time the most external and real-perceptible union with it" (*The Meaning of Love*, trans. Jane Marshall, rev. T. R. Beyer [W. Stockbridge, Mass.: Lindisfarne Press, 1985], p.93).

The use of erotic language had been nearly universal among mystics, including the most rigorously ascetic ones, but Soloviev was not expressing his views figuratively. On the other hand, he was far from antinomianism and equally far from an orgiastic disregard for the otherness of the divine. Needless to say, his influence has been slight, and maybe least within the church. However, echoes, if not of Soloviev then of the tendency he stood for, may be heard in Miguel de Unamuno's *Tragic Sense of Life*, trans. J. E. Crawford Flitch (New York: Dover, 1954). My otherwise much admired Thomas Browne even in his thirties lamented "this trivial and vulgar way of union—the foolishest act a wise man commits in all his life" (*Religio Medici* [1642; London: Dent, 1906], p. 79). All three of these moralists appear to have had happy and fruitful marriages. With regard to the Song of Songs, newer studies hold that erotic and mystical elements were united in its imagery from the beginning; see Arthur Green, "The Song of Songs in Early Jewish Mysticism," in *Orim* 2, no. 2 (1987).

8. The long history of the dealings of Christian churches with homosexuality has been recorded in detail by John Boswell in his book *Christianity, Social Tolerance and Homosexuality* (Chicago: University of Chicago Press, 1980). Boswell's now well-known point of view is that despite a claimed consistency of disapproval on the part of the church, there have been long periods of tolerance and even a praise of homosexual love among Christians, including the clergy. Boswell's thesis is contested by Fox in *Pagans and Christians* (see n. 5 above).

9. *Paradise Lost* 4:288–340.

10. *The Didache* 6.2, trans. Lake, in *The Apostolic Fathers*, (Cambridge, Mass.: Harvard University Press, Loeb Classical Library, 1912), p. 319.

11. See Phyllis Greenacre, "Conscience in the Psychopath," in *Trauma, Growth,and Personality* (London: Hogarth Press, 1953).

12. See Hannah Arendt, *Eichmann in Jerusalem* (New York: Viking, 1963).

13. On the surface, the quest for the origins of human hostility, as a primary or a derived set of intentions, may seem hopeless, since the evidence for one side or another is even less directly obtainable than our clues to the beginnings of guilt. However, as long as we do not think we must postulate an "instinct," as some sort of diffusable energy, it is useful, at least theoretically, to assume that the disposition to attack disappointing objects exists side by side with the desire to be one with gratifying objects. Such a pairing would be in conformity with survival. J. Lacan proposed that aggressiveness begins with the child's discovery through the agency of the mirror that its identity, its "me," is another being than itself as subject. See "The Mirror Stage as Formative of the I" and "Aggressivity in Psychoanalysis," in *Ecrits,* trans. Alan Sheridan (New York: W. W. Norton, 1977). Melanie Klein's *Contributions to Psychoanalysis, 1921–45* and many other works of hers support the idea of primal aggression, or the "death instinct," that Freud believed in.

· 4 ·

Concealing

It is a classic observation that we do not see ourselves as others see us. When Robert Burns prayed so fervently that by "some power's" intervention we might have such insight, he little reckoned what a disaster it could be. To have to put up with a self-estimation that would be the composite of one's friends' and fellows' opinions might be fatal. If we believed all the kind things our friends tell us about ourselves, we might be as badly off as if we believed our critics. Even criticism of one's published work sometimes contains enough venom that one's survival as writer depends on being able honestly and heartily to say it isn't so; how much worse an ordeal it would be to face a compendium of personal shortcomings. Of course, invidious critics might be wrong (one hopes so) as likely as right. Ordinarily we comfort ourselves with the belief that the consensus of opinion on our character is favorable, even if not so exclusively favorable as the standard obituary notice. But a requirement for well-being seems to be that we remain largely unaware of many things about ourselves that others can see, as well as many things that no one at all knows.

The truth of the matter is that the progress of our life enforces a steady discrimination between what we choose to notice, inside and outside ourselves, and what we choose to ignore. Note that I have said "choose," although it is easy to protest that there is no choice in the matter: for instance, I didn't deliberately go about ignoring the affront implicit in some words of mine, I simply said them "in all innocence," thereby compounding the concealment. Psychoanalysis, by insisting on close attention to the details of what I said, might reveal that I intended the malice and, further, that I intended to protect myself from noticing it. In short, when I refer to the "I" who acts, I am often referring to another than the one who carries out my actions with conscious purpose. We come back to Freud's "counterwill," and it is in this sense that we can speak of choosing.[1]

The listener whom I have thus unconsciously abused will recognize the malicious intent of the harmless-sounding words, and may also recognize my self-serving blindness. If he is exceptionally insightful, or exceptionally charitable, he will accept the slight in good humor and interpret my self-deception as further evidence of the limitations of human nature. Perhaps also he will be able, like a psychoanalyst at the peak of his form, to bring his interpretation to my attention, tactfully, leaving me enlightened and not resentful.

My example may be unfortunate if it suggests that our disposition to conceal our intentions and perceptions has a generally ignoble purpose—to preserve our self-esteem at the expense of others'. That is only one of the manifold intentions of the "defensive" measures we take (to employ that useful term of Freud's).[2] It is an example drawn from the everyday life of adults, and its chief use is to illustrate certain mental processes that go on all the time outside our awareness. Further, it reminds us that these processes are not the consequences of logic or of reason but rather of the profound unreason in our nature. The standards of logical thought that adults believe we adhere to, or would like others to adhere to, are conventions we have come to accept in the course of our maturation and education. We may be innately geared to a certain logic, if it is true that we are innately geared to a grammatical language of some sort.[3] But we must remember that our lack of true discrimination between what is inside and what is outside in infancy and childhood is an example of the peculiarities of all other mental functions, as well.

The sight of a mother or her breast or a feeding bottle can quell hunger for a while in her infant, the promise of gratification being an earnest of what is to come. The device will not work if it is too frequently not followed by actual feeding, but it is more than a conditioned reflex: it is the substitution in consciousness of an anticipated satisfaction for the desire itself. A contrary desire of infancy is to make something bad go away by not noticing it. How often do parents rely on their powers of distracting fearful, angry, or just bothered children by conjuring up something pleasant to distract their attention. Not only as children but also as adults, we rely heavily on our ability to forget.

The most urgent instigations to defense come from within. The example of the child who is distracted from hunger or irritability by the gentle ruses of its parents is only a kind of teaching model for more serious forms of concealment. Take that critical moment in the life of a child when the parents try to wean it from the nursing bottle to the cup, which is happily a less rigorous matter now than it was during the period of my pediatrics training. I recall a little boy from that time who was fed by cup instead of bottle once each day. He went along grudgingly, with loud protestations against the sacrifice, until one day he thrust away the beloved bottle violently, putting an end once and for all to what his parents were depriving him of little by little. He couldn't tell them so, but the inference was plain: better conceal the desire from himself than endure the agony of withdrawal.

Such a dramatic instance is unusual. The processes of concealment of desire, of turning away from fear, of splitting the self into knowing and not-knowing parts, of putting the bad outside and the good within (and vice versa), go on quietly, in innumerable minor cases. There are rewards, too, for such successful concealments—not only the visible reward of parental approval, but also the self-satisfaction that ensues from the mastery of desire or avoidance of fear. Parents reward their children mightily when they attain control of bowel and bladder, ordinarily by praising the achievement (although I can recall a time when some parents actually paid money for it). But the child has its own reward in the experience of being able to dispel the importunities of excretory function, not just in conforming to social demands. Being able to delay the fulfillment of desire is an acquired satisfaction in itself, as well as a way of avoiding censure. That all these concealments may also have unfavorable consequences is something we will consider later.

Analysts distinguish at least two principal kinds of avoidance. One is the denial of what might be perceived as coming from outside ourselves, the other the repression of inclinations from inside ourselves through the disappearance of the ideas that accompany them. Such distinctions have proven more valuable in theory than in practice, but it is unnecessary to pursue them here in a larger context of human nature. Distortion is of the essence of our experience of the world, inner and outer. It should hardly come as a surprise that we distort reality; it is a greater surprise, certainly, that we ever get anything straight. Few philosophical arguments have greater magnitude and tenacity than the argument over the possibilities of knowledge of the real world. We have to assume that the order we see in nature, including human and social nature, is an order of correspondence between reality and the linguistic structure, both biological and acquired, of our minds. Without such an assumption, we would have no way of being convinced that anything we said about the world, inner or outer, was more or less true than its opposite. It would take us too far afield to explore this idea in the philosophical depth it deserves. But we must always remind ourselves that our experience of what we sometimes call "reality" is a compromise. The sophist Protagoras was not wrong in saying that "man is the measure of all things," if he meant by that to proclaim the fragility of our certainties.[4]

The more we know about the world in which we "live and move and have our being,"[5] the more comprehensive is the reality, but no knowledge is incontestable.

I have summed up such concepts as denial, repression, distortion, and compromise under the heading of "concealing" because the effect, and we suppose the intention, of all these processes is to cover up whatever might conflict with our preferred state of mind. This is easiest to see when we are considering conscious emotional states. "When ignorance is bliss, 'tis folly to be wise" is a proverb that speaks volumes psychologically, although it bears the dangerous implication that blissful ignorance is always harmless. Not knowing about a potentially fatal illness at a time when it might be cured guarantees only a short-lived bliss. Failing to observe the inception of criminal behavior in a child is another such misapprehension. Never to think of the nuclear peril in which we all live may be blissful enough, but it paralyzes our will to take action against the peril. Never thinking of our own mortality, of the inevitability of our death, preserves us from conscious anxiety, but also from the deeper wisdom that comes of grasping our death as our own and holding it up to the promise of immortal life.

Notwithstanding the dangers of denial, it remains necessary to our existence that we do not pay heed to everything that comes our way. To be able to turn to art or music when one is suffering is a form of denial that is also a form of hope. Hope kept men and women alive as human beings even under the utterly degrading circumstances of the Nazi concentration camps, some of whose inmates formed symphony orchestras when they were permitted to, despite increasing anxiety about their lives. As their external surroundings worsened, even this hopeful form of denial failed or was taken away. Many of these people turned into living dead, seemingly shut off from any perceptions of their plight—a different kind of denial that is the result of total hopelessness. At least some of their tormentors in turn required the protection that Robert Jay Lifton calls "numbing": they were able to look upon their murderous activities as part of the day's work, after which they withdrew to the pleasant shelter of their homes and families and tended their gardens.[6] Acclimatization is also denial at times.

It is the inner flight from reality, however, that concerns analysts most. We have already seen that this flight takes the form of distortion as often as not. All socialization, all humanization, demands control of the hating, attacking, aggressive side of our nature that is at least potentially present from birth. I shall not contest the claim that it has greater strength in some of us than in others, simply because I am convinced that all our human and animal characteristics, including our capacity for concealment, are genetically directed. All of us to a greater or lesser extent have learned from experience, usually unconsciously, to apply the brakes to our passions, including the angry ones. The psychoanalytic contribution to knowledge is that such controls are not acquired absolutely or in perpetuity, but demand constant refueling and modification. "Beware the fury of the patient man" is another bit of folk wisdom that has relevance to us; his endurance of mockery, injustice, or intolerance may be limited after all.

Sometimes—often, in fact—an impulse to angry action must be consciously restrained. Suppose that we are the weaker party in a dispute and likely to bring on by action a greater retribution than we can handle, as is the case when we take on a governmental, departmental, or hierarchical authority. Or suppose that we are restrained by moral discipline from expressing just and effective anger, or that we have firm religious injunctions against injuring a neighbor. These are all conscious restraints, at least superficially. In the unconscious depths of our minds, restraints against hostile action or even angry thoughts can be automatic. We are unaware of the enormities of rage of which we are capable. Only under extreme stress, or under the illuminating inquiry informed by psychoanalysis or psychotherapy, do such impulses ever become apparent. The patient individual, free of even ordinary vindictiveness, who bears afflictions either stoically or with Christian forbearance, sometimes turns out to be capable of a violent animosity. We can often recover, step by step, the historical antecedents to such stoicism, but it is never really possible to distinguish finally between nature and nurture by analyzing. Since the intent of psychoanalysis as the historical study of the individual is not so much to explain as to relieve suffering, bringing about relief does not necessarily reveal that distinction. Rarely if ever can we pursue an analysis to the point where we have to admit that we have reached the bedrock of constitution; thus, it is best to assume the distinction as a given throughout. Seeming nonviolence of character is not, as a rule, preceded by parental threats or other punitive action against anger. Establishing habits of toleration or inner quietude in the face of provocation is possible under all sorts of environments in childhood and later life. The inner meanings of these habits will surely be diverse and related to the individual's experience, but the surface appearance of politeness, imperturbability, or even saintliness can be very similar in many contrasting life-histories.

One of the most obvious concealments is that of sexuality. Although the deeper psychological reasons for this concealment are outside our scope here, it is closely attached historically to religious values. The classical religious explanation—the discovery by Adam and Eve of each other's nakedness, and hence of their genital difference, after the initial act of disobedience—cannot be far from a psychological explanation. The account of the visit of a Renaissance pope to an Italian city, in which all the nude classical statues were for the first time modestly draped with fig leaves to conceal the genital organs, is both amusing and telling. This story illustrates only one of the ways in which sexuality is concealed. It acquires a certain poignancy in that the concealment was itself a kind of exhibition, for everyone must have thought: If the old man (it may be only a presumption that he was old) is so likely to be aroused, these statues must have been more provocative than we knew all these years! But for our purposes the story is only a paradigm: the instances of religious repression of sexuality are far more subtle. That the central figures of traditional Christianity are virginal has had a persistently repressive significance, since these models of divine humanity have shaped our ideals of life.[7]

The upshot of all this is that psychoanalysis considers man to be concealing and distorting by nature, as well as a loving, hating, striving, creating being. T. S. Eliot's observation that "human kind cannot bear much reality" gives the gist of what I am trying to convey.[8] Concealing is not an abnormality or a moral defect, at least not as I understand it here, but a necessary function of being in the human world. To acknowledge all reality, inner and outer, would be calamitous—even all of that little sector of reality that is ours to know. I should add, however, that it is not just a question of overload: we conceal selectively. The overriding principles of selection are the furtherance of satisfaction, the avoidance of suffering (except in instances where suffering itself gives satisfaction), obedience to sometimes undeclared moral standards, and perhaps above all—and most difficult to illustrate—conformity to preexisting convictions. "My mind is made up, don't bother me with facts" typifies the attitude that I refer to; the process it implies goes on without conscious intention. The "counter-will" has its own designs and it is according to them that much of our world is shaped.

We have already proposed that reality is not something given ready-made to us, but rather a world with which we come to terms, often through painful experience, when we recognize how it differs from our imaginings. On the other hand, we have also come to appreciate that our imaginings play a necessary role in the construction of our reality. It is not inaccurate to say that the whole business of analyzing is an unconcealing, a disclosure, and, in an interesting if limited way, a "revelation." By allowing oneself to saunter along these byways of thought, all manner of unexpected discoveries may be made. That is, we are capable of unconcealment to a greater extent than we ordinarily realize, not only without disaster, but with positive benefit. Psychoanalysis is only one way to become more conscious of the world, but it is unique with respect to the personal unconscious, our withheld world of intention, which can be so powerful in restricting us.

I would again insist that the concealed side of human nature is by no means only self-seeking. Such an implication would depend on an atomistic view of persons that is itself a distortion. To be sure, each one of us is bounded by the body and the continuity of the life contained in it, but to be human is to exist in relation to others, including those "others" contained in ourselves. Psychoanalytic study constantly amplifies this concept; in every word, every sentence spoken by patient and analyst, more than one self is speaking and being addressed. Although we rarely take it into consideration in our ordinary social conversation, our words are always matched to the inner picture we have of the person we are addressing. I must spontaneously change my manner of speaking to each person I address, partly on account of what I know about them, or how I know them, but also partly because of what I imagine them to be. In the close examination afforded by psychoanalysis, it becomes possible to recognize and demonstrate the hidden picture. The path to revealing what has been hidden by the denials, repressions, distortions, displacements, twistings, separations, and so forth leads through unconscious references to the analyst in the patient's discourse. The analyst must sort out who besides himself is being addressed in all these references, what remembered or forgotten person from the patient's past is invisibly present. The patient may unconsciously recognize the listener as an analyst, a doctor, a man or a woman, a parent or a sibling; all these many selves are present and hidden. When the analyst replies to the patient, he, too, does not address solely the individual recumbent on his couch, but also the lives being lived out by the patient.[9]

Perhaps the greatest concealment of all revealed by psychoanalysis is this secret multiplicity of individual human nature. We like to think of ourselves as unities, as integrated individuals; indeed, the word *integrated,* perhaps because of its affiliation with the virtue of integrity, strikes us as something we should want to be. As patients become freer to speak their desires, hopes, fears, and memories, they learn to assume the responsibilities of this multiplicity. It is not just a question of competing desires, but of whole representations of oneself that may be at odds with one another, yet are likewise capable of enhancing one another. I give the example of the woman who is a good wife and mother and yet is terribly unhappy about it. She feels put upon, degraded into being a household drudge, by sacrificing her life to her husband's socially approved dominance. It is a common enough modern predicament, often accompanied by guilt. The process of unconcealment exposes that woman's "other selves": perhaps an artistic vision that has been subdued or intellectual attainments that have given way to her husband's. This often painfully disturbing process also releases her sense of herself as one who, with less rage and guilt, can find ways of living out her hidden life while still enjoying motherhood and wifehood. Such a happy outcome is neither universally nor fully attained, but it is no small matter to see it as a possibility.

Concealment is not just episodic, like lying or other forms of conscious dissimulation. It is habitual, literally characteristic. Individual forms of concealment vary as do our other habits; indeed, they constitute much of what we consider our character and individuality to be. This is much more readily apparent in others than it is in ourselves. We wonder why this one is so self-effacing or that one so unnecessarily abrasive; at times we infer that these striking self-presentations are like masks behind which quite another sort of person is in hiding. It would be reductive of the infinite variety of human nature to suppose that once these masks were lifted, all that would remain would be the commonplace, psychoanalysis being a sort of human homogenizing process. Quite the contrary; as we try to maintain equilibrium in a social world that prefers the average to the exceptional, our masks are far more likely to conceal our particularity than our neutrality, even when they are striking enough in themselves. A new habit arises from the psychoanalytic process, that of speaking *oneself*. Its value, of course, depends on what that self has to say; so it is not without risks and does not lead to universal harmony. But we erect so many and such massive self-protective barriers that their dissolution, however partial, ought to make for a closer approximation of the Quaker ideal to "speak to that of God in every man." But that presupposes the belief, often understandably shaky, that God is listening behind the sullen, vindictive, or frivolous mask of the person whom we address.

I have sometimes compared our language to our skins, which grew with us as we matured and always fitted our bodies rather neatly, as our child's language grew to fit the requirements of later life. Like our language, our characteristic ways of being in the world, including our chronic concealments, have a proper fit that is difficult to recognize as anything but perfectly natural and seemly. People vary much in their capacity to stand apart from themselves and see the distortions that are special to them. It is a bit too much like looking at one's own eyes from within, presupposing as it does that the "self" making the judgment is undistorted. If this is true of our patients, it must also be true of us. One can see how unexamined qualities in our own characters might interfere with the work of analysts in elucidating the character of others. The ancient Delphic maxim "Know thyself" needs to be challenged by the yet more ancient Vedic question "How can the knower be known?" Our only answer is: With fear and trembling, and only a little at a time. This may be where Freud's phrase "the impossible profession" best fits psychoanalysis: it is truly impossible for analysts to be rid of the distortions through which we are required to see those of others. Any resolution of the ambiguity is specious; we are forced to accept that the understanding we seek to share with our patients is tentative, but perhaps that is as important an insight as any we have to offer.

To sharpen the Christian relevance of this psychological picture, I would like to consider the supreme act of unconcealment: the historical event of God's life with us on earth, as we understand it in the life of Jesus, and its sequel in his availability to us all the time. At the heart of the Christian faith is the revelation of the hidden One, the unseen Creator of all that exists—including our minds—who has worked within the evolving fabric of existence since the beginning and made himself known in Jesus. Every bit of fresh understanding that we gain of the created universe is a new evidence of God's unconcealment, as is every new insight into the meaning of Christ's incarnate life. We can never grasp or understand that life in its fullness. Mankind, even in the Christian dispensation, can neither stand nor understand this reality and tries again and again to conceal the redeeming Presence beneath all-too-human vestments, making out of our infinitely loving God a very human creature of power, pride, rage, and riches. I see an illuminating parallel between the psychoanalytical effort to disclose as much as possible of our deepest personal intentions and the ever-renewed Christian effort to show us the God who revealed and continues to reveal himself.

Notes

1. See chapter 1, note 7.
2. The concept of defense is all-pervasive in psychoanalysis, and I am doing it only partial justice in subsuming it under the title "concealing." I do so partly to be consistent with my program of presenting psychoanalytic ideas as descriptions of processes, rather than as causal explanations. I have also in mind that human experience is a constant alternation between awareness and unawareness; much of our motivation, as psychoanalysis understands it, proceeds without our awareness. Motivation unfolds not by being locked in static confinement in a dark attic, but by being transformed into something else, maybe its opposite. We remain fully, or even excessively, conscious of this in the form of symptomatic thoughts, feelings, and actions. Freud introduced the term *defense* and pursued it the rest of his life through a theory of energies that are denied expression and are either "dammed up" or transmitted along circuitous routes through the processes of defense. Such a metaphor has constantly tended to move psychoanalytical theoretical explanation into a discourse robbed of personal significance, quite unlike the dialogical discourse in which whatever is psychical emerges. The subject of defense is an enormous one; Freud wrote about it constantly and Anna Freud summarized the theory until 1936 in her book *The Ego*

and the Mechanisms of Defense, reprinted in *The Writings of Anna Freud,* vol. 2 (New York: International Universities Press, 1966). Anna Freud's title reveals a point of view I have tried to avoid, but she presented the phenomena with classic clarity.

3. See chapter 2, note 1.

4. According to John Burnet, "Plato more than once explains the meaning of the doctrine [of Protagoras as quoted in my text] to be that things are to me as they appear to me, and to you as they appear to you." See his *Greek Philosophy, Part 1: Thales to Plato* (London: Macmillan, 1928), p. 115.

5. Acts of the Apostles, 17:28. To be sure, in this speech attributed to him by Luke, Paul referred to God, not "the world," as the universal milieu.

6. R. J. Lifton, *The Broken Connection* (New York: Simon and Schuster, 1979).

7. On the virginity of Mary and Jesus, see Marina Warner, *Alone of All Her Sex: The Myth and Cult of the Virgin Mary* (New York: Alfred A. Knopf, 1976), and Leo Steinberg, *The Sexuality of Christ in Renaissance Art and Modern Oblivion* (New York: Pantheon, 1983).

8. T. S. Eliot, "Burnt Norton," in *Four Quartets* (New York: Harcourt, Brace, 1943), p. 4.

9. The recognition of the phenomenon of transference is inseparable from another fundamental psychoanalytic concept: the unconscious. The profundity of this insight cannot be exaggerated. Not least important, but too rarely commented on, is the role of language in the transference, which I have stressed here and in other writings. Verbal communication is a plunge into a common pool of language or, in another metaphor, a sharing of a jointly held treasury of language. Since we possess language in common, we are members of a community of mutual reference. It is from the fact of language that we know naturally that all of us are brothers and sisters, despite the "confusion of tongues" from which our enmities proceed. We say that language is "polysemous," that it is rich in meanings, and it is in that ambiguous wealth that we conceal and also reveal our feelings toward one another. Analysis of transference at its best is the skilled sifting out of hidden intentions in their emergence in the special discourse undertaken by two people; but we speak our hidden intentions to one another all the time.

· 5 ·

Suffering

Psychoanalysis began about one hundred years ago as a medical treatment for sick and suffering people. Freud, its founder, and Josef Breuer, the older man whose new uses of hypnosis were taken over, adapted, and later transformed by Freud, were both physicians with a special interest in neurology. At that time, neurology included not only the proven disorders of the nervous system (tumors and neurosyphilis, for example) but also the disorders of a less grave nature—of mood, anxiety, worry, restriction of pleasure and action—that were beginning to be called psychoneuroses. To a lesser extent neurologists were also concerned with the insanities, or psychoses, in which the psychiatrists (at that time often called "alienists") specialized. The theory behind this neurological approach was that there must be some abnormal changes in the nervous system to account for the sufferings and other symptoms experienced by "nervous" and "insane" people.

As soon as Breuer and Freud found out that the symptoms of psychoneuroses could be changed or even alleviated and apparently cured by hypnosis, they began to question whether these were nervous diseases at all—that is, whether they were symptomatic of lasting pathological changes in nervous organs.

Early in their work they were able to establish that the symptoms could rather be seen as disguised, distorted, or concealed repetitions of forgotten past events. A daughter's attendance on her sick father during his last illness, for example, came to be represented by terrors, paralyses, and muteness that cleared up when they could be traced with the aid of hypnosis to specific events during her care of her father, which they recapitulated in such a bizarre fashion.[1] That neurotic symptoms were disguised or concealed memories, or desires, became a psychoanalytic principle. As Freud's studies went on, the origins of these memories were pushed back further and further into the youth and childhood of the patients. It worked out that the lost memories of adult patients were themselves transformations of earlier memories, to which they had been tied by mutual affinities. To free someone of his or her symptoms, it was not enough to dispel them by recovering recent distressing memories; one had to put together the hidden connections in dreams and spoken thoughts that led into the remoter past. Psychoanalysis thus evolved into a system of making the past present by revealing the ways in which the past was repeated under concealment. It was in some respects a kind of archaeology, with the notable difference that what was "unearthed" was composed not of inert, broken sherds and monuments but of the living past.[2]

Note, however, that it all started as a medical procedure. Even Freud, early in his career, put his neurotics to bed at home or in nursing homes, gave them diets, prescribed medicines, sent them to spas for healing waters, and applied the impressive electric-spark machines that were in vogue around the turn of the century. How the care of all these forms of "nervousness" moved from religion, morality, superstition, and practical philosophy into the sphere of medicine is a fascinating story that I cannot begin to summarize here. A wonderful document from around 1600, Robert Burton's *Anatomy of Melancholy*, is a vast encyclopaedia that brings together the premedical and medical theories of mental anguish up to that time. What I find in Burton, along with all the quaint lore, the superb archaic diction, and the engaging little stories, is the unspoiled seriousness with which that solitary scholar took the varieties of suffering, as they were described in the European literature that was accessible to him. He wrote before the Enlightenment, when the scrutiny of reason began to be applied more rigorously, but also before technology, when individuals got lost in mechanistic categories. Although we cannot read such a book without constantly searching for familiar modern terms, nevertheless we are permitted to feel our way into the psychoneurotic experience as it was lived before the modern system of diagnosis was created.[3]

Freud worked in our era of medical technology. The definition and description of diseases were becoming more and more acute and discriminating. The great categorizations rested on a number of factors, including the microscopic and macroscopic pictures of diseased tissues and organs, and the isolation of causative agencies (or the preventive agencies in deficiency diseases). Positive measurable knowledge was at hand relating cause to process, course, outcome, and often cure or prevention of disease; this knowledge set the standards for inquiry into newer forms of evidence.

That psychoanalysis should become a positive science akin to scientific medicine was a genuine ambition of Freud's (although he by no means favored limiting its practice to physicians, as has until very recently been the official rule in America).[4] He wrote a small number of case histories that came to be models for all later studies of neurotic disorder, and to this day students of psychoanalysis are asked to look in their patients for the mental structures, conscious and unconscious, that Freud found in his. That his patients were all extremes of their sort, rather than typical, cannot be sufficiently emphasized, to my way of thinking. It is of great historical interest, for example, that as students we were introduced to the psychoanalytical study of obsessional thinking through Freud's great novelistic account of a young soldier who is driven to distraction by dwelling on a horrible torture inflicted with rats. But I question the usefulness of such a story in helping us to understand people who worry obsessively, let alone those who are over-scrupulous characters.[5]

I have permitted myself here to criticize a certain trend in psychoanalysis because, along with many other analysts and therapists of our time, I believe it has a far more valuable statement to make about human suffering and its treatment than imitation of medical practice permits. If we look on psychoanalysis as a deliberate, systematic attempt to understand the meaning of mental anguish in individuals and to relieve that anguish through the unconcealment of hidden intentions, we do not need to think in medical categories at all, or very little. In fact, we need be medical only in the sense of being able to rule out as unfavorable prospects for our kind of treatment those patients whose sufferings require more urgent methods, medicines, or even custodial protection against harming themselves or others.

To be sure, the ways of expressing mental suffering are to some extent classifiable and we are still able to use the old classification that Freud inherited and contributed to. Its usefulness declines when analysts allow ourselves to be guided by its diagnostic formulations to the point where we fail to see the patient who actually comes to us. It would be wrong to judge, in the interest of discerning individual differences, that there are no formal categories of disorder in mental suffering. It is another question whether they should be thought of as illnesses. Nowadays, when medicines are widely prescribed once more for all sorts of symptoms, we are likely to jump to the conclusion that whatever discomfort yields to treatment by medication must have been "caused" by a faulty action of the nervous system. Of course, that is not true invariably or even most of the time; it is possible to banish cares and sorrows for a while with our most available drug, alcohol, but nobody would contend that the troubles so relieved were organic in nature, except as all experience is mediated by the nervous system. Occasionally we have the opportunity to observe both kinds of disorder, presumably organic and psychological, in the same person. Successfully analyzed patients whose lives following their treatment give ample evidence of the efficacy of the analytic experience—especially by assuming tasks that had hitherto seemed beyond their capacity and engaging in more enjoyable pursuits—nevertheless may have periods of anxiety, for example, that are better treated with medicine than with further psychoanalytic treatment. On the other hand, to believe that the effects we ascribe to psychoanalytic self-observation over a long period could be wrought by medicines is akin to believing that one could learn Chinese or write music by taking pills.

Whether mental sufferings are medical or not, they are genuine sufferings, as real as the pain of fracture, inflammation, or tumor. They differ from physical disorder in a significant way, however: they gradually shade into either the ordinary troubles of life or the spiritual concerns without which no one is truly human. To be anxious about a sick child, to be plunged into sorrow by a bereavement, or to be preoccupied with the concerns of business are all ordinary responses to the contingencies of existence in this less-than-perfect world; not to have such responses would be to lead a flattened life. At the other side are our spiritual concerns. Are we living up to our ideals? Are we doing all we can do to relieve others' suffering? Are we as conscious as we could be of God's presence? Do we ever love enough? And do we forgive honestly and fully enough? These are a different set of concerns from neurotic worries, while not always fully distinguishable from them.

Both sets of concerns, ordinary and spiritual, shade gradually into the disorders that analysts treat. It is by no means always easy to decide whether "normal" troubles ought to be treated as symptoms in the psychoanalytic sense of the word, such as a grief that time does not lessen, or a solicitousness about a child that is destructive of the child's progress toward adulthood. There are no hard and fast rules, no laboratory tests. The professional is liable to err in diagnosing all kinds of suffering as symptoms of disorder requiring treatment. On the other hand, the professional is less likely to make the suffering worse by increasing the patient's shame and guilt, as may happen when troubled people are told they are being foolish or selfish in worrying so much, or merely advised to pray more. As a professional who knows that we do sometimes make too much of our normal woes and fail to take advantage of spiritual resources, I still believe that analysts and therapists have much to offer in helping people to decide whether they need treatment.

This question of suffering exercises the Christian conscience in every generation. To look on it as a question that can be answered, so that it need no longer be asked, seems wholly wrong. Such an intention leads sooner or later to skepticism and despair or to utopian solutions and the consequent effort to force human nature into predetermined molds, to create a new order of mankind, as if the process were something like calendar reform or the introduction of the metric system. How many such attempts we have found in western history alone! All insist that by enforcing certain changes in the conduct of society we will cause a new humanity to come into being. All the great atheistic political revolutions of our time have projected the liberation of mankind from suffering, but through political and social methods that were effected by means of general disruption and mass murder. Psychoanalysis has not been part of their programs. The Soviet Union, after first welcoming psychoanalysis as a revolutionary new approach, then proceeded to outlaw it when it turned out that the analysts really meant what they were talking about, really intended to help people express themselves, which cannot be permitted in a closed society. Christian utopias have also designed programs to do away with human suffering through the formation of a devout, purified community, separated from the evil world. If the psychoanalytic picture of discontented and striving humanity bears any resemblance to the truth, it should be plain that failure is built into such attempts.

But my profession has had its private utopias, too. It is one thing to support the goal of preventing disorder. If we could establish that this or that kind of mental suffering had a common background in the upbringing of children, in practices that have had unsuspected, long-term deleterious effects, then it would seem not only reasonable but urgent to take measures toward eliminating the causes of this suffering as we understand them. Unfortunately, a program of prevention is by no means ready to hand on the basis of our knowledge of the human psyche. Even the broadest of proposals, like recommending that every child have good parents—one so general that it hardly requires the special wisdom of psychoanalysis to offer it—need qualification in the face of the circumstances of life. Since there cannot be more than one pair of natural parents, it is usually necessary to make do with what is available; trying to change parents according to a program of preventing disorder may end up by making more bad parents. More specific ideas like the breast-feeding of children, engaging both parents in child rearing, early or late bowel training, spacing of siblings, rewards and punishments, acquiescence to childish wants, and programs of education—all of these have to be considered, but no program is certain to succeed. Attempts to prevent future malaise by what might be called "technical" measures are sure to ignore the host of other actions, attitudes, and events that make up the tangled web of human growth. I must add, in partial qualification of my cautions, that I find among the present generation of young parents a certain ease in the handling of their children that was conspicuously absent in the preceding generation. It may be that these young people have had good reason to doubt the efficacy of the programs conjured up by their and our predecessors and prefer to apply love and commonsense in less complicated or systematic ways. Or, optimistically, it may be that they have made their own the sounder principles that their parents applied with awkward good intentions. The new spontaneity cannot be equated with the "natural" program of upbringing of the past, which was often governed by quite severe and dogmatic positions.

In short, my experience drives me to a profound skepticism

about our ability to take concrete actions to prevent neurotic suffering. It, like physical disorder, is likely to remain with us, although in both cases we ought to adopt all measures that seem to be of potential benefit in reducing suffering and prolonging life.

It is not out of order at this point to raise the question whether psychoanalytic understanding sheds any light on the mystery of human suffering. I think that it does in certain specific ways, although they are not necessarily the unique findings of psychoanalysis. They may be found in other statements of earlier ethical positions. I have already mentioned them in describing the analyst's view of human nature. But why, if we learn some of the reasons for neurotic suffering, and can even treat it more or less effectively, can we not prevent it? An answer may follow from what has been said before in this discussion. Human desires are limitless, and human powers of concealment are, too. The root of neurotic pain lies in the fact that all sufferers distort their desires out of the basic human incapacity to fulfill them. To put it in simplest form: because we cannot always have what we want, we pretend to ourselves that we want something else. As I have said, the effectiveness of psychoanalytic treatment is based on that assumption: through the discourse, the dialogue, the sufferer penetrates his own disguises, speaks his desires. That does not guarantee their fulfillment, but it frees him of their distortions. Freud's wry comment that psychoanalysis changes neurotic suffering into ordinary misery may not sound too hopeful, but it is a candid appraisal of man's fate.

In connection with the limits of our ability to abolish suffering, I should like to mention what has been so often called in religious circles the "value" of suffering.[6] Perhaps because Christians acknowledge and give thanks in the Holy Eucharist for the sufferings of Jesus, they are sometimes disposed to assert that all suffering has redemptive value. Granted that we may find the redemptive moment in our ills an additional confirmation of God's presence or a turning to the greater suffering of others, the value is not in the suffering but in the rescue from it. Preventable suffering is not meritorious; quite different is the assumption of pain in the imitation of Christ, for the benefit of others.

Behind all this is the sobering fact that it is our coming into the world that disturbs our peace. Moved out of the antenatal equilibrium, we become strivers, our striving only briefly stilled by periods of gratification. The restlessness of which St. Augustine wrote is the source of our suffering; it is also the source of all our efforts, movement, and productivity, and of all efforts to mitigate our lot. I find that I cannot do without this paradoxical statement of our situation. To be human is to be caught in a paradox; that is the mystery of our natural being. It is neither an optimism nor a pessimism. One of the outgrowths of liberal thought is the conviction that there are, or ought to be, remedies at hand to ease man's fate. Within limited horizons, that is true: the prolongation of life through modern medical care is one irrefutable example, and our slow and spotty progress toward eliminating poverty and infectious disease speaks in its favor. But the dissatisfaction of the individual with his lot is not to be overcome by social measures.

I have never analyzed anyone who was satisfied with his or her parents or siblings. To some extent the dissatisfaction is itself a distortion produced by the method of analysis, in which the patient is being listened to by an imaginary parent who is, for the time being, free of the limitations of actual parents and is easily idealized. But what emerges is the criticism, complaining, rage, and sorrow about one's upbringing, mirroring the deeper levels of one's lifelong grasp of the family. It may be paralleled by love, humor, and compassion, but the shortcomings of those who raised us or were raised with us, given the opportunity to voice them without reproach, are magnificently plain.

There is worse to come. Our lifelong inner dissatisfaction with and complaints about those who were the first members of our world do not go unpunished. Indeed, the sufferings endured in all the distortions and concealments are in great measure the products of guilt. By the nature of our development, the parents who gave us life, loved us, protected us, trained us, and inevitably disappointed us have also planted in us, or caused to grow in us, the sense of wrongdoing from which we cannot fully escape, whether our parents themselves are alive or dead.

Our inner struggles concern not only our self-imposed concealments, our inability to know what we want, but also these internalized voices that have become parts, if often fragmentary parts, of ourselves. It isn't just conflict and suffering that these parts of us produce. Our sense of justice, decency, and propriety can act as a positive guide to living. Freud's discoveries confirm Hamlet's "Conscience doth make cowards of us all," but they also show us how conscience makes heroes of many. All overcoming of temptation is the work of conscience, except insofar as it is the work of mere prudence. None of this is new except for the psychoanalytic claim that conscience proceeds not only consciously but also unconsciously; in its unconscious form it may both diminish our happiness and actually engage us in bringing about unnecessary misery. The unconscious conscience, like a bad parent, punishes vindictively. In the guise of wishing to be "good," we may indeed refrain from doing bad, but also from doing anything pleasurable, good or bad. On the other hand, the unconscious conscience may foster the most rigid self-righteousness, the kind that inspires others to mischief or desperation.

All this is no doubt familiar enough, but I wish to sketch in this abbreviated form the Freudian psychoanalytic picture of man in his inevitable inner conflicts. "Man is born to trouble sure as sparks fly upward" is as true a proverb psychologically as it is existentially. What I hope to affirm, then, in this very limited story of the roots of mental suffering is some psychoanalytic insight into the human condition as it is, not as we might wish it to be. Man is a discontented animal. In anticipation of what will follow, it is pertinent to recall that the critics of religion, both within and outside psychoanalysis, often and tiresomely charge that we are religious because of our unhappiness, trying to make up for the woes of life with beliefs in a life to come, a beneficent savior, and so on. We ought not protest too vigorously against such charges. They contain the Christian truth that the church from its beginnings has always preached: that it is out of our unhappiness, our fear, our guilt, that we can recognize the gift of salvation.[7] In the end, the only difference in this respect between the fathers of the church and its critics is that for the critics salvation is a fantasy, a mirage, while for believers it is the gift of God through Jesus Christ. The critics are quite right in supposing that a fully satisfied human, with no failures, no sense of wrongdoing, no griefs, no fears, no longing for the eternal, would have no occasion to look to God. But it is they who are indulging in fantasy when they imagine such a creature and suppose it to be human.

Notes

1. This is the case of "Anna O.," first undertaken by Josef Breuer in 1880 and later conducted by Freud. As I suggest later in the text, this and other cases have become paradigmatic for all instruction in the theory and method of psychoanalysis; they have also been subjected to a kind of reanalysis many times, and in some instances, as in that of Anna O., the later history of the patients has been unearthed and related to the original accounts. This case was first published in Breuer and Freud's *Studies on Hysteria* (1893–95) and is found in the *Standard Edition* of Freud's works, vol. 2, pp. 21–47.

2. For discussion of the archaeological analogy in Freud's writings, see W. Schönau, *Sigmund Freud's Prosa* (Stuttgart: J. B. Metzlersche Verlagsbuchhandlung, 1968); D. Anzieu, *Eléments d'une théorie de l'interprétation*, *Revue française de psychanalyse* 34 (1970), pp. 755–820; and my *Psychoanalytic Dialogue* (New Haven: Yale University Press, 1980).

3. Among the many excellent histories of psychiatry and psychoanalysis are Henri F. Ellenberger's *Discovery of the Unconscious* (New York: Basic Books, 1970) and Reuben Fine's *History of Psychoanalysis* (New York: Columbia University Press, 1979).

4. The question whether the practice of psychoanalysis should be limited to doctors of medicine has been constantly troubling since psychoanalysis came to the United States; in Europe, including England, it has been

more readily assumed that other avenues of experience prepared the practitioner, as well.

5. See Freud's "Notes upon a Case of Obsessional Neurosis" (1909), in *Standard Edition*, vol. 10. It would be captious criticism to mention only the shortcomings of this and the other case histories. They are not only all we have by way of clinical studies by the founder of the field; they are also masterpieces of observation and inference. It is often not recognized that they point far beyond themselves into ways of thinking they do not themselves encompass.

6. Unamuno, who had a grasp of our spiritual nature second to none, accompanied by an intense realism, nevertheless wrote so extollingly about suffering as to embarrass his admirers: "Suffering is the substance of life and the root of personality, for it is only suffering that makes us persons. It is the universal or divine blood that flows through us all. That which we call will, what is it but suffering?" (*The Tragic Sense of Life*, trans. J. E. Crawford Flitch [New York: Dover, 1954], p. 205).

The allusion to the divine suffering, central to Christianity, is developed further, but Unamuno's baroque exaggerations, taken seriously, seem to encourage not just the endurance of human suffering but its exacerbation or neglect. To the extent that he opposes suffering to indifference, he is of course right, but well-being offers still other spiritual possibilities. He wrote these words before the First World War, and long before the Spanish Civil War.

Unamuno's point of view is not uncommon in religious writings and gives rise to the suspicion that Christianity teaches the enjoyment of pain, or "masochism." For a contrary opinion, see "How Did Jesus React to Suffering?" by Fr. Claude Ortemann, in *Cross Currents* 36 no. 1 (1986).

7. The Christian message is one of appeal to the poor, the suffering, the wretched, the oppressed. A modern "liberation theology" has grown authentically from this appeal. But everything we know about Jesus shows that his call was to everyone and that "all ye that are heavy laden" included rich and poor without distinction. Jesus, while he did not praise suffering (see preceding note), recognized its universal presence, as who of the people who wrote the Psalms would not? Buddhism, too, began with this recognition. It has remained for the modern culture of universal happiness to base all its hopes in this world.

· 6 ·

Believing

I have analyzed very few believers in any religion, although most of my patients were brought up as at least nominal Christians or Jews. As a matter of fact, on the basis of the many case histories that I have read or heard, it appears that relatively few believing and observing Christians and Jews come to be analyzed. I am aware that this is a pseudo-statistic, because I have also discovered that many analysts fail to take their patients' religion seriously into account. This omission nowadays has various roots, one of them being that most men and women trained as analysts have not held to religious convictions of their own and therefore have not been made impressionable to those of others. They may suppress the appearance of religious sentiments or sometimes fail to recognize them out of ignorance. In other instances they are moved by delicacy or discretion: religious differences have so long been used as reasons for unfriendly discrimination that it might seem wiser or more just to avoid any mention of them. It may also be that my observations are only pertinent to psychoanalysis in the strict sense in which I have used the word, leaving out the greater number of patients treated in a psychotherapy informed by psychoanalysis, but I don't think that this explains the scarcity of religious patients. The most probable reason is that members of the educated and professional classes, who constitute the great majority of our patients, have given up serious religious belief and practice well before they came to be analyzed.[1] Carl Jung, in his 1937 Terry Lectures at Yale, made his often-quoted remark that believing Christians were protected against neuroses by their faith, a position that I would be very happy to confirm if I could do so honestly.[2]

These considerations do not relieve me of an attempt to present something of the psychoanalytical understanding and critique of religion and to add my explanation for the prevailing irreligion. I shall begin with an infrequently noticed paper by Freud, many of whose conclusions about the nature of religion have become authoritative psychoanalytic opinion. This is a little article first published in English in 1928 under the title "A Religious Experience."[3] It is the reply to a letter sent to Freud by an American physician who had read a statement of his about his "lack of religious conviction and . . . indifference towards survival after death." The American lamented Freud's unbelief and related an experience of his own as a young medical student. One day he had seen in the dissecting room of the hospital the dead body of an old woman, whose sweet face made a profound impression on him. "The thought flashed into my mind: no, there is no God; if there were a God, he would never have permitted it that such a dear old woman would end in the dissecting room."

The young man, who had for some time entertained doubts about Christian teachings, at first resolved never to enter a church again; but then "a voice spoke in [his] soul" urging him to reconsider, and he decided to wait to see whether some sure conviction of faith came to him. In the course of a few days, that is exactly what happened. "God made it clear to my soul that the Bible is God's word, that all that we have been taught about Jesus Christ is true, and that Jesus is our only hope." He went on to express his wishes for Freud's conversion, which he repeated in a further letter in response to Freud's courteous but firm reply that he expected to remain "an infidel Jew" unless God should accord him a similar inner voice—an event for which not much time remained, in view of Freud's advanced age. I cannot help praising the article for the quiet and friendly if also ironic tolerance of a point of view with which Freud profoundly disagreed, and which in this instance he even attributed to a hallucinatory experience.

Freud went on to explain the religious experience as a reliving of the Oedipus complex. In chapter 2 I presented this essential Freudian concept of our psychic structure as the dynamic residue of our passionate relationships with our parents in childhood, its typical form being found in the boy's powerful loving attachment to his mother and his jealous, often rageful antagonism against his father. To Freud, the young American student's experience could be explained as a return of the ancient passionate triangle, with his mother represented by the corpse of the sweet old lady and his father by the malicious God who had deprived him of her. To abandon belief in God was to kill his bad father. But the forces of submission to his father, also surviving from the primitive constellation of the family, overcame the initial rebellion. The voice, a psychotic hallucination, was overpowering and the rebel surrendered, his recovered faith in God being a repetition of his surrender to his father as a little boy.

Freud's article is so short that it is perhaps unfair to present it in this abbreviated form. I offer it here not so much for itself, but as an example of a certain principle of the psychoanalytic interpretation of religion that is made sharply clear in so unpretentious an example. It may serve as a paradigm, providing we remember that Freud was "analyzing" a letter, or rather an experience reported in a letter, with only the barest recourse to the associative method of psychoanalysis. The Oedipus complex, all the same, is one of our working hypotheses, one of our rules of interpretation. This means that it forms part of the structure of the analyst's attention to what the patient is saying. The Oedipus complex has its basis in the psychic reality of childhood life (I don't see how that could be called an "objective" reality) and is not just a shared fantasy of analysts. We are ever on the lookout for evidences of its presence, in countless transformations, in the thoughts of our patients.

Having said so much, let me add that I believe Freud was right in the way he put together the elements of the American doctor's story. The old woman's sweet face may well have reminded him—unconsciously, as far as we can tell—of his mother, and the God who had ordained the woman's death and permitted what seemed to be the indignity of autopsy may have been for the student a prohibiting, avenging father, who himself deserved to die. Where Freud fails us, on the other hand, is in his too ready conviction that the underlying, obligatory psychic structure rigorously determines the whole conscious content of experience. There we see psychic determinism in its cruder form, a determinism that leaves no room for anything new to happen. It is one thing to claim, as analysts do, that the persisting structure of the personality laid down in early childhood experience frames our organization of later life; it is another to see in the experiences of life only disguised repetitions of what has gone on before. Now, repetition is also a basic psychoanalytic idea, implicit in the concept of the structure of mind, but as that most questioning of modern analysts, Jacques Lacan, reminded us in one of his more lucid statements, repetition is not reproduction, but a transformation into which events outside one's own life have been likewise integrated.[4] In the case of the American doctor we need to assume that the force of religious doctrine, and the contingencies of his life, found a soil prepared by his childhood experience. From the Christian point of view, the seed fell on fertile ground. We need not depart far from our clinical experience to construct equally plausible but opposite outcomes; indeed, far more frequently than not, we observe the outcome of the ancient oedipal struggle in the abandonment of religious faith and observance, but here, too, we have to see something more than a mere repetition.

The American medical student's story brings us to a critical position. If we grant the psychoanalytic explanation (after making generous allowances for the insufficiency of our information and for the mere shadow of a psychoanalytic situation), and if we further acknowledge that this seeming repetition of the Oedipus complex bears within it a complex network of personal meaning, where, then, do we make contact with the religious experience as it was reported? And this brings us to the question: "Was it the voice of God?"

How often and how variously the claim has been made that God has spoken to men and women! It is essential to remember that all psychologies, to the extent that they make any scientific claim, stay within the realm of earthly experience to describe and try to explain the workings of the mind. Psychology cannot encompass the divine within its parameters. From the experience out of which I write, the two orders of existence—earthly and divine—are equally real and interactive; but we must be content in this life to keep them intellectually apart, in the hope that in the life to come, when we shall see face to face, they will be unified without needing intellectual bridges. Such a seeming dualism is repugnant to many in our age. Faith in God, and especially in particular instances of God's interventions in individual lives, is comfortably abolished when we provide psychological explanations that leave nothing inexplicable. But it is equally possible to make psychological explanations conform to religious doctrines, in the interest of avoiding the dualism. An eroding away of scientific categories of understanding then takes place, rendering legitimate criticism impossible. That ought to dissuade us from adapting psychology to religion, popular as it is among believers. When I wrote that in the case of the medical student "the seed fell on fertile ground," pious reflection might imply that I introduced the parable of the sower by way of accounting for what had happened to him. But I used the familiar metaphor within the context of my story, as Jesus did in the context of his own original and quite different one.

It is regrettable that the psychoanalytic critique of religion began with a persuasively written antireligious tract, Freud's *Future of an Illusion*.[5] It established a position that has been taken as the official view to which Freud's followers subscribe. Because of its author's preeminence, the book and the point of view that it embodies carry the weight of the clinical and theoretical writings on which psychoanalysis rests. Stripped of its polemics, the argument as it has developed runs something like this: Since our lives do not always proceed according to our heart's desire and often go in quite the contrary direction, we avail ourselves of our capacity to imagine, so as to create an unseen world in which we can ultimately obtain what we want. It is hardly wonderful that the personified representation of this ultimate benevolence should be located in our good mothers and that our "heaven" should be envisaged as a restoration of those sheltering arms, those munificent breasts. Likewise, it is reasonable to hold that we adhere to the belief in an omnipotent law—one that sustains the universe but also imposes its rules, moral as well as physical—out of our awe before our powerful fathers. That these parental roles are often mingled, or even reversed, presents no objection to the thesis. It is readily demonstrable from the analysis of dreams and fantasies that we do unconsciously transform our memories into images and imagined situations that fulfill our wishes but owe little to the real world outside ourselves. Any imagined situation is therefore likely to emerge from this wish-fulfilling potential, since even in our waking lives we are by no means in command of unconscious mental processes. In these ways we become able to endure, even enjoy, the renunciations exacted of us by life.

This argument sounds more plausible when we are contemplating another religion than our own. Pagan weather-gods easily strike us as evidences of wish-fulfilling fantasies: what could be more convenient than having at our disposal methods of inducing rain or sunshine by dance and incantation? Even in monotheism, the erotic satisfactions of a Muslim heaven are transparently desirable, if only from the masculine point of view; and it was typically Jewish for the rabbis to conceive of a heaven in which the faithful (once more the men) spend eternity studying Torah with God himself as exegeticist. Buddhist aspirations to absorption in the limitless sea of spirit, freed of all the contingencies of existence, are for us the longings of a wearied people deprived of hope. And within Christianity we may readily dispose of sectarian differences as vain imaginings— the devotion to Mary as seen by Protestants, for example, or any orthodox view of Christian Science. Nor need we try to confute the analysts by pointing to the retributive element in our faith, the threat of damnation: that, too, can be admitted as wish-fulfilling, once we give due allowance to the universal longing for chastisement that, like the spankings or admonitions of childhood, restores us to the good graces of our divine Parent.

Why, then, should we be less receptive to the Freudian contention that in our prayers and liturgies we are invoking powers that are the imaginary product of our deepest needs and desires? And how can we face the Freudian claim that in these efforts we evade the human and moral responsibility of trying to solve the problems of life by our own efforts, turning instead to an unseen divinity to perform what we cannot be sure of doing ourselves? And, above all perhaps, do we deliberately blind ourselves to the inevitability of death by positing a heaven or even a hell in which we shall continue to live? These critical questions strike me as deserving serious attention by Christians because they point to actual conditions in the lives of believers, even if we can finally show them to include basic misunderstandings of what our religion is about.

However, before we look into such matters, a few more elementary criticisms of religion from the psychoanalytic position deserve our notice. Freud observed rather early that religious rituals resemble the formal and repetitious practices of certain sufferers with obsessional disorders, who are obligated to enact ineffectual procedures of various kinds over and over again.[6] In fact, it is Freudian custom to name such obsessional practices "rituals" and to see in them a curious commentary on what we do in our ceremonials. Like the obsessional person's commitment to a perfect performance of his handwashing or dressing, or his elaborate sexual preparations, the religious observer, priest or layman, needs to go about his or her actions according to rigidly prescribed forms, convinced that omissions may nullify the efficacy of the operation. Can it be, Freud asked, that religions are public neuroses and neuroses private religions? Once more, it will be noted that Freud's contentions strike us as more plausible when we think of others' religious behavior than when we think of our own. Literature is full of references to the peculiar behavior of Jews either in the synagogue or praying singly with their strange phylacteries stretched on their arms and foreheads. And how odd it is that Catholic Christians go through all those processions and genuflections, and that Moslems lay out their little rugs towards Mecca! The worst of it is that each of them finds the others very obsessional, once they lay hold of the jargon of psychopathology.

In his remarkable study *Group Psychology and the Analysis of the Ego,* Freud compared churches with armies. In both, the success—and maybe the survival—of the group depends on leadership. The ideal leader is just that: an ideal, someone who can serve as the bearer of the highest values of all his followers. They in turn are united in merging their differences within the person of the leader; he is their common best self and for his sake they help and serve one another. Furthermore, because they see him in their fellows, they absolve one another of fault. All is in the interest of unity of purpose. Such is the state of affairs in the church or army at its best—"best" from its own standpoint, of course. A necessary consequence of this unity, as well as one of its preconditions, is that all disruptive tendencies find targets outside the group, since such tendencies—hatreds, jealousies, suspicions, objectionable desires of all sorts—are not eliminated by the harmony of the group. Someone must be found to be the enemy, the scapegoat, who helps maintain the unity of the group by being the externalized bearer of its disowned evil. Corroborating examples of this description within the Christian fold are so many that I shall not belabor the point by specifying any of them. Freud added a comment that is no less important (although not to the present consideration): namely, that what looks like a growth of religious tolerance in modern times (the book was written in the twenties) may well mean not a growth in charity but only a decline in religious fervor. Oddly enough, Søren Kierkegaard said the same thing in the middle of the nineteenth century.

In these extracts from Freud's writings on religion, I have restricted myself to a few that seem to me to have genuine usefulness and interest to believers, despite their uncompromisingly antireligious tone. Freud's respect for religion was shown by his lifelong interest in it as a human concern, but evidences are short that such respect was of a different kind than his regard for other human frailties. What I have selected, however, are ideas that grew from his close attention to human nature, and therefore have a validity that does not depend on the truth of the antireligious stand that may or may not have motivated them. As a matter of fact, in *The Future of an Illusion*, Freud candidly remarked that his reflections on religion, intended to be negatively critical, might just as well be put to another use by believers.[7] That is precisely my intention; I hope that I do not seem to be in the position of the devil quoting Scripture.

To Freud, a man of the Enlightenment—to which we are indebted for so many of the better things in our social order— religion was a holdover of the childhood of the human race. He predicted that a mature humanity, after long growing pains, would rid itself of this bit of infantilism and accept with something like equanimity that we are alone in the universe, more or less the playthings of fate. Freud believed that our only hope lay in self-knowledge, which would perhaps mitigate our sufferings in the long run by enabling us to confront the realities of our existence. It was in the strength of that conviction that he and many of his followers applied themselves to the "scientific" study of religion and came to conclusions of which I have given some illustrations—or rather, discovered psychoanalytic explanations for what they already firmly believed. Another powerful encouragement to rationalist atheism came from

· 78 ·

the religious climate in which Freud grew up in early twentieth-century Vienna. Whatever comfort the dominant Roman Catholicism of Austria might have given its adherents, it meant to Jews of the time only a repressive, obscurantist hierarchy and discrimination against them in all stations of life, as well as a consistent opposition to intellectual investigation that might lead in dangerous directions. This is not so far from Christian behavior in our own age and country that we should find it hard to credit. But Freud, while remaining a member of the Jewish community, was equally critical of his ancestral religion, seeing its monotheism as being a step ahead of earlier paganism, but no less doomed to extinction with the advance of science.[8]

Christians attempt to answer Freud in two or perhaps three different ways. The easiest is to denounce psychoanalysis as false, devilish, "pansexual" (borrowing the preferred adjective of Pope Pius XII), or in some other inclusive invective. It is part of the irreligion of modern life, exactly as it claims to be. In a roundabout fashion, the condemnation has reappeared as a scientific criticism, disposing of psychoanalysis with the magical word "unscientific." Christians had better steer clear of that term, because the "scientific" criticisms of religion can put the psychoanalytic to shame. The mechanistic-materialistic view supposedly derived from physics and chemistry disposes of religion more readily than of psychoanalysis. Faith in God is even less acceptable to these hard-headed scientific skeptics than is the unconscious. The second defense of religion is more difficult because it requires the Christian to know what he or she is talking about: this is the careful, sometimes line-by-line examination of psychoanalytic texts, undertaken with the earnest intention of demonstrating how they can be fitted with Christian meaning. Thus, we could try to make a correlation between Christian charity and sublimated sexuality, or between the "aggressive instinct" and sin. Another version of the same method is to put the concept of "basic trust" (in one's parents), very persuasively put forth by Erik Erikson, on a plane with our trust in God.[9] Or we can turn to Christian purposes the concept of the "transitional object"—convincingly devised by Donald Winnicott to account for the child's attachment to, say, the rag doll—and thus have a forerunner for the adult's attachment to the invisible parent symbolized by God.[10] But notice that all such attempts aim at preserving the intellectual respectability of religion by forcing it to submit to a secular language. Through them religion can be shown to mean something equally accessible outside its domain. The skeptic now can sit at ease with the believer (like the lion with the lamb, but only after the repast) knowing that he is dealing not with delusions or even illusions, but with "metaphors," which are after all only a matter of taste.

Such modesty on the part of believers strikes me as uncalled for. It leaves out of account the prodigious claims of revealed religion and almost, if not quite, obliterates the testimony of religious experience. According to any traditional Christianity, certain events are on record as having occurred that are taken to be no less than the explanation of the world. A people on pilgrimage, having fled from the land of their bondage, met with experiences that bore the unmistakable signature of God and were assured of his very presence before them. Later some of their number recognized the divine presence among them, as a man among men and women. These critical events, symbolized by Mount Sinai and Mount Calvary, have determined the direction of the Christian faith, because the memory of them has been transmitted through the generations as of immediate concern to them all. So my third way of answering Freud's criticism of religion is governed by faith. We have every respect for the psychoanalytic findings that go into the "explanation" of religion; after all, there must be some human pathway through which whatever we know of the divine can be mediated. The human status of faith faces believers long before they come to think about psychoanalysis. For example, what is the status of often-contradictory religious texts as warrants for belief? Is any of them literal history, factual reporting? But all the documents are contestable and have been contested. Belief requires that one make up one's mind by assenting to a claim as it is presented. As for the believing community, does its claim to unbroken continuity reckon with other traditions that failed to survive because God was, so to speak, on the side of the big battalions? Whoever wants to see his or her faith in the light of history must come to some convictions with regard to these and many other questions.

So, too, with the history of individuals. In examining applicants for postulancy to the priesthood, I have met with a large number who have suffered the loss of their fathers in childhood and early youth. This is no accident. Certain analytic hypotheses (or maybe just commonsense) suggest that it is not a remote speculation to suppose that the postulants' religious vocations had something to do with their losses. Parallel observations are common enough, but to consider the "explanation" definitive— implying that a limited number of events, usually disastrous ones, in early life instigate the religious quest—is only to the purpose of treating religion as a symptom.

Faith rests on tradition, but tradition rests on believable experience. Something held to be of supernatural origin happened to someone, who convinced someone else that it happened; otherwise there would be nothing to believe. Skeptics are, thank God, permitted to believe and say that what really happened was hallucination or another private experience to be accounted for naturalistically; but that need not alter the faith of the believer, although the believer must acknowledge that religious hallucinations and delusions do exist. The mass suicide of the inhabitants of Jonestown in Guyana must not be forgotten or ascribed too easily to the cynical machinations of the cult's leaders. The point is, however, that religious faith within its own horizons has its basis in a reality that is not confined by the subjectivity of the individual. The believer (who may, like Blaise Pascal, be of a skeptical turn of mind) recognizes that the truth he or she assents to resembles a relationship with someone more than it does a scientific hypothesis. Like such a relationship, it turns to an *other*. Religious faith exacts a recognition of one who *is*.

We turn also to personal experience of the kind that is usually called "mystical." Properly understood, this is a valuable category, but the term has come to isolate such experience as something quite apart from the common life. There have existed an immense variety of mystical experiences and the accounts of them are numberless; alongside the conviction that the heart of the story is beyond communicability, many mystics seem to have an urgent need to communicate it. Hans Loewald has written about the experience of timelessness: "Philosophers and theologians have spoken of the *nunc stans*, the abiding now, the instant that knows no temporal articulation, where distinctions between now, earlier, and later have fallen away or have not arisen. All of us know, I believe, poignant moments that have this timeless quality: unique and matchless, complete in themselves and somehow containing all there is in experience."[11] The author of this relatively simple statement does not profess in it any religious belief at all, but he has described what is for many one of the grounds of faith. The sense of timelessness runs counter to all ordinary experience, in which we are normally conscious on reflection of the passage of time. In living outside time, we exist also in a world that is not bounded by the sight, sound, touch, smell, and taste of the world in which we carry on our daily life; we often feel the presence, though not with any of our senses, of a being on whom we are dependent. When that is analyzed as a clear repetition of our childhood sense of dependency on reliable parents (or a single parent), we ought not necessarily to dismiss the analysis: it was Jesus, not Freud, who said, "Ye must be as little children to enter the kingdom of heaven." The experience of which Loewald wrote is one that comes to light infrequently during psychoanalyses, not, I believe, because it is so rare, but because we are trained by our whole culture to ignore it.

But mystical experiences such as the moment of timelessness

or the conviction of unity with nature, the human world, God, or Christ, constitute only one form of the directly religious encounter, although I believe they are more important and more frequent than is recognized. There are also flashing instants of compassion, when we know we must drop what we are doing and come to the aid of someone in pain or other distress. There are convictions of right action, when we know that we have to do works of love regardless of our own safety and well-being. It is, of course, not only Christians who have acknowledged such calls to genuine martyrdom, to bearing witness to the truth, as countless examples attest.

All this has been said better and with urgent clarity by an eminent biologist, G. E. Hutchinson. In his autobiography, *The Kindly Fruits of the Earth*, he writes:

> The subjective intuition of the presence of God seems obvious to me, though of course saints and mystics have it to an incomparably greater degree than do most of us. Some people do not recognize it, others unhappily are taught to ignore it. I have no idea what the solution to the questions that the intuition raises, such as the problem of the existence of evil, may be. This ignorance, however, is not an exceptional defect. I am aware of the explanations in objective terms that can be given for the intuition. None of them explain why that which is supposed to underlie the experience translates subjectively into what is experienced. As far as I can see the problem raised by any such translation is, in principle, insoluble. We do, however, possess a capacity for metaphor which seems to absolve us from total silence in the face of that of which we cannot speak. Such metaphors may hint at formal relations without being available as bases for logical deduction. All theology to me consists of metaphors, some less totally inadequate than others.[12]

The "subjective intuition of the presence of God" is one of the private but far from rare experiences that our religious convictions rest on, and they should not be devalued by any explanations that psychoanalysts can give. In fact, where analysts (not excepting Freud), have shown a certain obtuseness has been in their triumphal announcements that all our religious experiences have forerunners in our personal history and thus do not mean what they claim to mean. Do they require us, as the Egyptian taskmasters required of the Israelites, to make bricks without straw? It is from the straw of parental love, of conflicting desires, of suffering, of hopefulness, and of the language in which we conceive all these, that the bricks of faith are made. Having the lives we are given to live, when we hear the Gospel of Christ we know that it is spoken to us and that it transforms us. Or, it does not, either not now, or not in this life.

I promised to offer a few thoughts about why religious belief seems to be on the wane in our time. I can claim expertness for my ideas only if they are drawn from my experience as psychoanalyst and psychiatrist. What is more, anything said on the subject needs to be qualified by the observation that the waning of belief is only noticeable among a certain large class of people with a fairly advanced Western education. Everyone else in the world goes on, cheerfully or grimly, with one or another form of traditional religion, or an occasional new one. That some religions are very grim indeed I need not remind anyone in this day of religiously dedicated suicide-bombing. But I have learned from my patients, and from others whose lives have been narrated to me, that "some people do not recognize" religious experience, while "others unhappily are taught to ignore it." When Hutchinson wrote those words, he was not entering a plea for prayer in public schoolrooms, and he would look on what is ignorantly called "creationism" as neither science nor sound religion. Rather, he was reminding us that the modern intellectual habit of mind avoids the disturbance that arises when we admit the possibility that the still, small voice that we hear is God's and that the world in which we live is full of evidences of his presence. In addition to the justifiable revulsion the educated and compassionate must feel when they think of the many horrors wrought in the name of religion, there is a certain attitude among intellectual people with regard to religion that

I can only call snobbery—not the worst human fault, but hardly anything to be proud of.

Among intellectual people in our day, atheism and agnosticism bear much the same cachet that orthodoxy has borne in other times. The French describe people who are properly and often snobbishly orthodox as *bien pensants*, meaning "right-thinking." One might call the term a slightly off-color variant of "orthodox"—off-color because it implies pretension. Among the bien pensants of any persuasion, it is indecent to refer to those who maintain a contrary opinion, except with ridicule. Be sure that I am not denying the existence of a genuine atheism, the kind that Martin Buber said was another form of worship of God because it expressed dissatisfaction with all our approximations of him.[13] Atheists of that kind are always eager for discussions and disputes with us, because they know that the topic is all-important. In some ways Freud was of that serious class of atheists, but many of his followers have been simply snobbish and unwilling to risk their complacency, or perhaps their professional standing, by looking too closely or personally into the question.

All these considerations notwithstanding, we have good reason to be sympathetic with the unbelief of many of our contemporaries. As I have tried to understand why unbelief is the normal position among the educated, I have found Freud's explanation true enough in many respects. Liberation from the dominance of parents is a necessary part of "becoming" a person in one's own full being. Even to take over the valuable characteristics of one's parents, quite as much as to become immune to the less valuable, demands a process of liberation. The determined questioning of all given values can be exasperating to the parents of adolescents; but it clears the way for the assumption of responsibilities of one's own. Religion is so deeply intertwined with childhood dependency, and in particular with sexual immaturity, that to be on one's own may require, or seem to require, abandoning the parental faith, or for that matter any faith. The discovery that one does not really have to be religiously observant, or sexually abstinent, may be the first step toward personal freedom. For liberation to take place, the young man or woman draws on the support offered by the unbelieving world outside the family. When belief was the rule in educated circles, such support was less available, although it could always be found. I suspect all the same that the "ages of faith" were in reality ages of enforced conformity and compliance, with more insincere belief than one finds today; worldly rewards for religious conformity are now scant. Yet it would be a misreading to infer from these thoughts that freedom must mean loss of faith. Rather, it means putting serious questions to religious authority, and this implies distinguishing between religious authority and God. W. H. Auden, who understood these matters with exceptional clarity, wrote concisely: "Every Christian has to make the transition from the child's 'We believe still' to the adult's "I believe again'." This is a necessary transition. "In our age," Auden goes on, "it is rarely made, it would seem, without a hiatus of unbelief"—if indeed the "hiatus" does not become a permanent state.[14]

All I can contribute to understanding the modern unreligious attitude of intellectual people is to see it as a widespread fashion. That it is transitory I think is proved by the increasing groundswell of oriental religion among the young. By appropriating aspects of Buddhism or Hinduism or Islam, it is possible to assert one's share in a community of faith, without having to subscribe to the still suspect traditions of one's ancestors and neighbors.

Notes

1. The predominance of well-educated patients in the clientele of psychoanalysts can be misleading if it is inferred that it requires intellectual knowledge and high intelligence to undergo psychoanalysis successfully. This was not true in earlier days, and it need not be so now. Nevertheless, two circumstances dispose in favor of this state of affairs: first, that the time and money that psychoanalysis demands can be afforded by only a favored few; and second, that the mystery surrounding psychoanalysis serves as a barrier for the uneducated.

2. C. G. Jung, *Psychology and Religion* (New Haven: Yale University Press, 1938), p. 52ff.

3. Freud, "A Religious Experience" (1928), in *Standard Edition*, vol. 21.

4. J. Lacan, *The Four Fundamental Concepts of Psychoanalysis*, trans. Alan Sheridan (New York: W. W. Norton, 1978). H. W. Loewald, too, distinguishes "re-creative repetition" from "passive, reproductive repetition" in his study "Some Considerations on Repetition and Repetition Compulsion," in *Papers on Psychoanalysis* (New Haven: Yale University Press, 1980), p. 90. For all the limitations of the "ego-psychology" that for a long time exerted a constricting influence on psychoanalysis and offered mainly empty tautologies as explanations, it nevertheless had the healthy effect of turning our attention away from the fascinations of the past toward the problematic present and future. Psychoanalysis is indeed concerned with the past, but in its *thematic transformations*. It raises not only the question "What from the past does this manifestation represent?" but also "What has the person made of his or her past?"

5. *Standard Edition*, vol. 21. This is the longest essay by Freud devoted to religion. There is much more material in his *Civilization and its Discontents* (ibid.), *Group Psychology* (*Standard Edition*, vol. 18), and elsewhere, including of course his very late *Moses and Monotheism* (*Standard Edition*, vol. 23). Freud evidently thought that his "godlessness" was essential to his psychological discoveries. To be sure, a religious adherence that entailed submission of independent ideas to a reactionary authority would hardly have fostered Freud's radical questioning. A recent presentation of this point of view has been made by Peter Gay in *A Godless Jew* (New Haven: Yale University Press, 1987).

6. "Obsessive Actions and Religious Practices" (1907), *Standard Edition*, vol. 9.

7. The passage deserves quotation in full: "Nothing that I have said here against the truth-value of religion needed the support of psychoanalysis; it had been said by others long before analysis came into existence. If the application of the psychoanalytic method makes it possible to find a new argument against the truths of religion, *tant pis* for religion; but defenders of religion will by the same right make use of psychoanalysis in order to give full value to the affective significance of religious doctrines" (*The Future of an Illusion, Standard Edition*, vol. 21, p. 37). Freud's generosity is not quite evenhanded, since "affective significance" is no substitute for "truth."

8. Attempts have been made to turn the psychoanalytic tables on Freud to explain why he was an atheist. W. W. Meissner's is the most detailed and sympathetic, drawing abundantly on Freud's writings, as well as external information. It is plausible enough, but no more convincing, that the convictions of a believer can be "explained" on the basis of his or her childhood

experience. See Meissner's *Psychoanalysis and Religious Experience* (New Haven: Yale University Press, 1984).

9. E. Erikson, *Identity, Youth and Crisis* (New York: W. W. Norton, 1968), p. 82: "The ontological source of faith and hope . . . I have called a *sense of basic trust.*"

10. See Meissner (n. 8 above); D. Winnicott, "On Communication," in *The Maturational Process and the Facilitating Environment* (New York: International Universities Press, 1965), esp. p. 184; and A.-M. Rizzuto, *The Birth of the Living God: A Psychoanalytic Study* (Chicago: University of Chicago Press, 1979).

11. H. Loewald, "Comments on Religious Experience," in *Psychoanalysis and the History of the Individual* (New Haven: Yale University Press, 1978), p. 65.

12. G. E. Hutchinson, *The Kindly Fruits of the Earth* (New Haven: Yale University Press, 1979), p. 79.

13. "But when he, too, who abhors the name, and believes himself to be godless, gives his whole being to addressing the *Thou* of his life, as a *Thou* that cannot be limited by another, he addresses God" (M. Buber, *I and Thou* [Edinburgh: T. and T. Clark, 1937], p. 76). Much of the philosophical direction of my book is grounded in the position so vigorously and devoutly stated in *I and Thou*, another early discovery for which I have been thankful for a lifetime.

14. W. H. Auden, "As It Seemed to Us," in *Forewords and Afterwords*, selected by Edward Mendelson (New York: Vintage Books, 1974), p. 518.

·7·

Ending

As much as anything else, it is the knowledge of death that defines our humanity. That we shall die, that everyone will die, and that all the things that concern us must also end sometime—this finitude, mortality, temporality stands as the limit that cannot be transcended through any effort of our own. Language and tool-making, it is said, we share with other animals; at least we do if we accept broad enough meanings of those words. I am among those who also believe that animals have subjective experience and a wide variety of feelings, not just sensations. But the ability to conceive that there will be a time when we shall have ceased to be appears to be uniquely human. The most important fact about the idea of dying is that we don't like it and that as humans we never have liked it. Our Neanderthal ancestors colored the bodies of their dead with red dye, the color of life, and all subsequent peoples have shown, through ritual burial, grave goods, and monuments, that they wanted the lives of their dead to continue or resume.

It has been remarked innumerable times that our unwillingness to accept death as extinction is no evidence for immortality. It may be only part of that determined struggle to stay alive that has kept us going through the hardest of times; the desire for life has survival value like nothing else. It makes us almost infinitely resourceful, so that in our effort to preserve our own lives or the lives of those we love, we sometimes have powers we could not otherwise expect of ourselves. We refuse to die and so, confronted by the inevitability of death, we imagine another life and are on the lookout for any and all confirmatory evidences of it. On the other hand, like other such skeptical insights, this one can be reversed, and we need to remember that the desirability of immortality should not militate against its existence any more than for it. Immortality is not rendered impossible just because we want it so much or, for that matter, because there are those who say they do not want it.

Psychoanalysts generally agree with Freud's dictum that there is no idea of death in the unconscious. What does that mean? If we think about the manifest content of dreams, we know that we do indeed dream about death and dying. We see dead people and at times wake in dread when we are confronted with the danger of imminent death. But even in dreams, which are conscious in themselves, although they have meanings of which we are unconscious, the dead awaken before our eyes, long-dead dear ones return nonchalantly or with wonderful welcome, and we ourselves may die and then continue living. Dreams aside, there is another way in which we know that death is not a final limit: we are as subject to the influence of persons long dead as we were when they were alive, maybe more so. This is no less true when we consciously repudiate their teaching and example. In a way, the absence of an unconscious idea of death is equivalent to the absence of time in the unconscious, also noticed first by Freud. In discussing belief, I quoted the psychoanalyst Hans Loewald, who related the timelessness of the unconscious to the mystical experience of timelessness.

It is only in this negative way that believers might claim support in psychoanalysis for any of our doctrines of life after death. We might propose that since, in this deepest part of our minds, death does not exist, we take it as evidence of our knowledge of immortality. The trouble with such an idea is that the unconscious side of our mental life seems too untrustworthy as a source of what really exists. Every possible paradox, inconsistency, incongruity, and absurdity endures in that realm of mind, and if we were to use it for our standard of reality, we would soon be out of touch with the rest of humanity. On the whole, psychoanalysts have opposed doctrines of immortality. Their antireligious bias is a partial reason; but belief in immortality also could be a variety of self-deception, one that interposes an agreeable fantasy in place of the grim reality. By this reasoning, fantasy is what we want, reality is what we get, and reality demands that we renounce our desires in large measure. Lately, if my impressions serve me right, the assurance of psychoanalysts on this and all religious subjects has weakened a little, which might mean that psychoanalysts have come to recognize the metaphysical limitations of their science and have also seen that the positivism that restricts reality to the evidence of our senses falls far short of describing the human condition.

It would be reasonable to think that a matter of such importance as the inevitability of death would loom large in the discourse of any analysis. When we are telling "what comes to mind" without censorship, surely this drastic, ineluctable horizon should confront us often and correspondingly influence all that we say. Surprisingly, this is not so. We can remember the deaths of others, as part of our past history or as events occurring during the analysis. The deaths of individuals who have played a large part in our lives may turn out to have been determinative events, as I have remarked earlier; deaths and funerals during analyses are often occasions for the revelation of hitherto concealed feelings and fantasies. But the prospect of our own death comes up for consideration only under special circumstances: when some possibly life-threatening physical symptoms have not yet been definitely diagnosed as benign, when we plan long plane journeys, or when we write wills (and that, too, usually takes place when we are under some external pressure).

As a matter of fact, whole analyses may take place with outcomes satisfactory to both patient and analyst and no mention be made of death. It is as if immortality, far from being the vain imagining of the religious, were already a normal expectation within ordinary life, not on the other side of a mysterious threshold. Many years ago, the respected psychoanalyst Lawrence Kubie wrote a short article in which he warned us that we must begin to prepare for physical immortality (I think that freezing the body was the method then proposed); we would have to reorganize our expectations around this anticipation.[1] I didn't think of it at the time, but I might well have replied that the conduct of our mental and spiritual lives already prepared us better for physical immortality than for the actual certainty of death, since we lead our lives, in and out of psychoanalysis, as if we were never going to die.

This has not always been the case and probably is not the case everywhere even now. Johan Huizinga, in his book *The Waning of the Middle Ages*, wrote of the omnipresence of the ideas of death and dying in the late medieval period.[2] Closer to our time, in the early part of the nineteenth century, the high infant mortality tempered the joys attending a new birth by the likelihood of early death; and the fierce attrition caused by tuberculosis among young adults became part of the standard environment of Romanticism, as well as the setting for many religious conversions. In such periods—and these are only two striking examples to which many others could be added—the shortness and fragility of life could not be concealed for long, however much we are disposed to do so.

To isolate the modern theme that relegates consideration of our dying to emergencies only, I must call it a symptom of hopelessness rather than a sign of the healthy mind. Nor may I call it the wisdom that Spinoza praised when he said: "A free man thinks of nothing less than of death, and his wisdom is a meditation not of death but of life." [3] How can it be that we are free or wise if we live out the imaginary prospect of having limitless lives on earth? It seems to me rather that true freedom and wisdom require as full a recognition as possible of the reality that death imposes. It is very likely that we withdraw from this recognition *because* we have come to have no hope for an existence beyond that of our natural bodies, and because we have got rid of the supernatural. Having abandoned hope for life outside time and space as we know them, we feel better off pretending that we shall not die.

Looked at in another way, this pretense isn't surprising at all. I discussed earlier the process of "concealing." If we hide from, distort, or ignore whatever is distressing, and if death is the most distressing prospect, then it is natural enough that we avoid mentioning it even in analysis, when we are bidden to tell whatever we are thinking. That is, we don't think about it. That there is no unconscious notation of death supports our avoidance. The concealing devices of our minds, being themselves unconscious, shield us by screening out the reality of death. This ultimate limitation to all earthly desire is lost in the noise of more immediate concerns. Assisted by the great prolongation of life through modern medical means, we can almost persuade ourselves (or so it seems) that new remedies will always be arriving in the nick of time and that we, as individuals, will be spared. Thoughts of death are not like our hidden sexual desires that leap into our discourse from the unconscious sources that eventually make themselves known.

One of Freud's few theoretical proposals that has not found universal favor with his followers has been that of the "death instinct." [4] Without discussing it in detail here, I need only remark that it fits logically with the view that we seek gratification of desire and that in fact all our efforts intend the gratification of desire. But the end of such satisfaction would mean the absence of desire and accordingly the absence of intention, which is death. Such is one line of the reasoning that led Freud to postulate the death instinct. An early follower of

Freud noticed the similarity of this view of death with the nirvana of Buddhist religion. Stress on the end of desire, and therefore on the end of pain and disappointment, is common to both views. I understand of course that there are differences, too. Other supposed evidences for a death instinct include self-destructive urges, both conscious and unconscious, and the unconscious need for punishment.

It has always seemed an affront to evolutionary theory to propose an instinct which at its flowering would mean not the survival that all our other instincts promote but the disappearance of the species afflicted with it. It is difficult on the face of it to imagine just what it would mean for a species to include in its genetic composition a pressure for gratification that would lead to death in advance of successful reproduction. Nor has the picture been clarified by the juncture in theory of the death instinct with the "aggressive" instinct, by which the former is interpreted as the turning inward of the latter. I confess to a certain attraction nevertheless to the theory of the death instinct (to the extent that I can accept any instinct theory in psychoanalysis) whenever I reflect on international politics in the age of nuclear destructiveness: such considerations make me ask whether it might not be that the human race is tired of existence and for that reason does not undertake to safeguard itself better than it has done. That aside, the death instinct strikes me as redundant and really quite impossible as a concept. It is antievolutionary and runs counter to the evidence in all animate beings of their constant attempts, whether ingenious or desperate, to avoid and outwit death. The most suicidal preoccupations, as psychoanalysts above all have pointed out, have in view the discovery or recovery of a better life, even if it needs to be beyond the grave.

It is rather in certain other directions that psychoanalysis has a contribution to make to our thinking about death, about ending. They lie in the psychology of concealing—that is, of the denial of death, of mourning, and of the preparation for one's own dying. The denial of death has become a commonplace of modern discussion; witness all the euphemisms we employ in talking about death and dying, to the mortuary customs that try to obscure the corruption of the flesh, and even to the misuse of religious language, by which the hope of immortality and resurrection is supposed to take the place of grief. None other than the redoubtable St. Jerome was an early and principal offender in this latter respect, when in a famous letter he chided a Roman Christian mother for mourning the death of her young daughter.[5] Jerome would probably not have ventured to act so if he had not known that it is indeed possible to suppress grief, just as it is possible to conceal other emotions if we have good enough reasons for doing so. One of the more remarkable events in the course of many psychoanalyses has been the discovery of a lost or hidden grief. This is more striking sometimes when the loss has been that of a parent in one's early childhood. Very young children manage this most terrible loss by "thinking of something else" far more effectively than adults can. Unhappily, the loss is no less real because it has been "forgotten," and the devices for keeping it unconscious themselves become parts of the character. They are not necessarily all, or always, bad parts of the character, but when a person has neurotic symptoms, the habit of denial or of covering up may make up part of the symptoms.

The psychology of mourning, which is the opposite of the denial I have just mentioned, holds that mourning is an activity (a "work," Freud called it) that follows naturally on loss if it is not impeded by cultural or neurotic inhibitions.[6] We part unwillingly with the beloved, and cannot do so all at once. It is no exaggeration when the bereaved cries out that he or she has lost part of the self with the death of the partner, because our loving attachments, as we have seen, are mutual transfers of selfhood to a greater or lesser extent. Every fresh memory of the lost love reminds us of our affliction, and pains anew. But it does little if any good, despite the tactfulness of our well-wishers, to try to keep the memories out of mind. We need to come back to them again and again, each time confronting ourselves at once with the loved presence in memory and with the finality of death. The comfort of religious faith may be great and always ought to be at hand for the believer, but the outpouring of feeling, far from being irreligious, is the signature of love. Step by step, the lost loved one is surrendered, without loss of either love or memory, but also without blocking the achievement of a new love. C. S. Lewis, an Anglican writer not often associated with psychoanalysis, wrote a highly pertinent little book about this process after the death of his wife.[7]

Our psychoanalysis is rarely content to leave things on such a positive note without an accompanying reminder of our liabilities. For we have to remember that the lost love was not exclusively loved. In another connection I mentioned the disposition to blame those with whom we are closest for their failure to fulfill all our expectations. When a beloved person dies, he or she cannot ever again make up for the dissatisfactions that we have felt in their conduct toward us. In fact, the very business of dying somehow strikes us at some center of our being as an affront. Was there ever a widow or widower who did not have the thought, "Why did you leave me just when I needed you most?" That, however, is only the most obvious part of the negative aspect of grief. Freud taught us to see that the self-reproaches of mourning may represent reproaches to the dead person, redirected against oneself. Here, too, we see the result of human closeness: if you are no longer there for me to tell you your shortcomings, your downright hatefulnesses, then I will find them in myself; for were not you and I one person? With good fortune, and aided by a certain candor towards ourselves and also, if necessary, by sympathetic counsel, this side of grief, its most painful side, is mitigated by time and living, as we come more fully to accept the limitations of our human nature. Here if anywhere we should be able to do better in the presence of God than we could by ourselves. The mystery of death is not less but more of a mystery for believers; refusing to accept the totality of the ending, they can seek and obtain forgiveness, in hopeful anticipation of a further enlightenment.

A comment of Loewald's seems remarkably apt in this connection. It was made to illustrate the phenomenon of "internalization"—that is, the process whereby we may overcome even the most minor or inevitable losses by changing ourselves after the model of the person we have to forego. Trivial and transitory examples of internalization of this kind often occur when we briefly take on, without conscious imitation, mannerisms of someone we admire, as children (and sometimes adults) do with movie actors, public figures, sports heroes and heroines. Sometimes, too, we find that our highest ideals are embodiments, so to speak, of other persons whom we have admired. In a way, all of us are the result of many such internalizations, not least being the characteristics of our parents that have become a part of us. Loewald reminds us that this tendency has a very special Christian value:

> It seems significant that with the advent of Christianity, initiating the greatest intensification of internalization in Western civilization, the death of God as incarnated in Christ moves into the center of religious experience. Christ is not only the ultimate love object, which the believer loses as an external object and regains by identification with Him as an ego ideal. He is, in His passion and sacrificial death, the exemplification of complete internalization and sublimation of all earthly relationships and needs.[K]

I believe that Loewald omitted one theological requirement in this observation, namely, the resurrection of Jesus. We can hardly believe that this "internalization" of Christ, this taking of him into our hearts to be our highest self, would have come about if some trustworthy followers had not been convinced that they had seen him and talked with him after his death. To that extent, we believe in him not solely because he, our leader, was put to death. Nevertheless, it helps me and may help others to grasp this radical piece of *Christian* psychology if we can relate it to one of the most familiar experiences in the life of the mind—the appropriation of the lost loved one into ourselves.

And with what a profound understanding has the church taught us to refresh that internalization through the Eucharistic meal![9]

T. S. Eliot summarizes much of this for us in his poem "East Coker":[10]

> Old men ought to be explorers
> Here and there does not matter
> We must be still and still moving
> Into another intensity
> For a further union, a deeper communion
> Through the dark cold and empty desolation,
> The wave cry, the wind cry, the vast waters
> Of the petrel and the porpoise. In my end is my beginning.

Notes

1. I have been unable to trace this reference.

2. J. Huizinga, *The Waning of the Middle Ages* (New York: Garden City, 1954). See also P. Ariès, *Western Attitudes toward Death: From the Middle Ages to the Present*, trans. P. M. Ranum (Baltimore: Johns Hopkins University Press, 1974). Ariès concludes his study by comparing ancient and modern ideas of death, saying that "death has become *unnamable*. Everything henceforth goes on as if neither I nor those who are dear to me are any longer mortal. Technically, we admit that we might die; we take out insurance on our lives to protect our families from poverty. But really, at heart we feel we are immortal. And surprise! Our life is not as a result gladdened!" (p. 106)

3. *Ethics*, part 4, prop. 67. Unamuno makes the psychoanalytically cogent comment that Spinoza's statement bears the marks of a "vain endeavor to free himself from the thought" of death (*The Tragic Sense of Life*, trans. J. E. Crawford Flitch [New York: Dover, 1954], p. 31).

4. See especially *Beyond the Pleasure Principle* (1920), *Standard Edition*, vol. 18. For all the problems raised by this concept, it warrants serious reflection, especially when taken in connection with human destructiveness in general.

5. Jerome *Letter 39*, trans. W. H. Fremantle in Philip Schaff and Henry Wace, eds., *A Select Library of Nicene and Post-Nicene Fathers*, 2d ser., vol. 6 (Grand Rapids: W. B. Eerdmans, 1954), p. 49ff. Jerome begins his letter to the griefstricken mother of Blaesilla with seeming sympathy, but is able to call her tears "detestable, sacrilegious, unbelieving."

6. S. Freud, "Mourning and Melancholia" (1915), *Standard Edition*, vol. 14.

7. C. S. Lewis, *A Grief Observed* (London: Faber, 1961).

8. H. W. Loewald, "Internalization, Separation, Mourning, and the Superego" (1960), in *Papers on Psychoanalysis* (New Haven: Yale University Press, 1980).

9. A brief phenomenological study summarizing the complex network of ideas within the structure of the Eucharist is E. S. Casey's "Commemoration in the Eucharist," in A. de Nicolás and E. Moutsopoulos, eds., *God: Experience or Origin?* (New York: Paragon House, 1985).

10. T. S. Eliot, *Four Quartets* (New York: Harcourt Brace, 1943).

· 8 ·

Reflecting

It is time to reconsider. I un-
dertook to write about a psychoanalytic view of man, always
keeping in mind our belief that man is made in the image of
God. It may be difficult to find that image in the struggling,
conflicted, suffering, anxious creature that I have portrayed. I
don't think that is all I have portrayed, but psychoanalysis is
concerned mainly with those aspects of our existence. It is the
sick, we are told, who have need of the physician, and as it
turns out, psychoanalysis reveals that the sickness is universal,
although present perhaps to a greater degree in some than in
others. But is this the whole picture, the whole image of God?
Many may assert that the image of God ought to be something
else, something more like the newly created Adam of Michel-
angelo, waking to life at the inspiriting touch of his Maker, with
the rest of creation awaiting his participation and mastery. I
might avoid this criticism by reminding you that the psychoanalytic view presents man as he is in the "fallen" state that
Christians also claim for him, man whose freedom—which
constitutes his humanity—has been abused. I do indeed avail
myself of this argument, but there remains more to say about
man's reflection of God, man's being truly an image of God,

that is far from fully obscured by his fallenness. Do we see through psychoanalysis any of the qualities of the divine, any of the markers of likeness to God? I shall consider this question in concluding this study.

Ludwig Binswanger, a friend and follower of Freud, complained that Freud paid too little attention to the spiritual side of life. Freud's reply, like the one he gave to the American doctor, was characteristically ironic: he said he was too busy with the lower, basic structure of our minds to have the time to dedicate to those loftier levels.[1] In truth, as I have suggested, Freud and many of his followers have believed that the spiritual, especially in its religious forms, can best be understood as a disguise for infantile concerns that have been denied transformation into maturer forms. I have attempted to show, in discussing belief, that this position grows out of antireligious prejudice and is not necessitated by any psychoanalytic findings.

Many Christians and Jews, and maybe more who have abandoned affiliation with any religious communities, have found in Jungian psychology a support for their spiritual lives, and it may well be asked why I have not taken Carl Jung's psychology into consideration. To all outward appearances, his writings are so pertinent to religion and never are marked by the lofty intellectual condescension toward it that makes the writings of Freud—and of most Freudians—on the subject unacceptable to believers. Jung was directly interested in religion, or, more properly, in religions, with particular respect to their symbolism; he and his followers worked out a system of symbolic representations that unified the unconscious values of many religious systems. While they made allowances for the cultural and historical differences among the religions, they also showed that unexpected similarities reflect the basic need of humanity to turn to God (or to the gods). To derive the support of religion, it does not appear to be essential to have faith in the sense of committing one's trust to the claims made by a religious community that it is the bearer of revelation from outside the human world. On the contrary, according to Jung, the symbols of religion are part of our universal unconscious equipment. There is no necessity to believe that these symbols have arisen out of concrete historical experiences like an actual revelation on Mount Sinai or at Calvary; they are self-authenticating and they make religious observance legitimate, with or without commitment to any revelation from God himself.

Jung—a pastor's son, whether he was himself a believer or not—at least had some serious firsthand acquaintance with Christianity, as well as an extensive knowledge of many other religions that probably ran deeper than Freud's knowledge of Judaism. Why, then, have I neglected to introduce the ideas of Jung more intimately into my account? I hoped to anticipate this and similar questions when I maintained at the beginning of this book that there is room for an indeterminate number of different understandings of human nature, and hence of different psychologies. It is likely that in applying a variety of psychological principles and methods, we shall make different psychological discoveries. All that one can honestly hope to do is to present an inwardly consistent understanding as a practitioner of one system without dismissing all the alternatives. I suspect it will turn out that many of Jung's discoveries can be brought into coherence with those of Freud, or vice versa; old personal and political (and even quasireligious) loyalties on these matters are dying out with the passing of the generations, and it is doubtful that anyone has a monopoly of the truth.

All the same, I do not feel it as a deficiency that I am less acquainted with Jung's psychology than are some of my friends who have made it the center of their study. Whatever the shortcomings of Freud's system—and I have not dwelt on many theoretical objections—it seems to me to take into account with marvelous thoroughness the complexities of the human situation, from birth through development to maturity, old age, and dying. As I have presented it here, it concerns itself with love and hope and fear, with care and envy and jealousy, with ambition and competition, and with making the best of the desperate condition into which our lives are often thrown. Those and similar concerns strike me as significantly parallel to the liveliest religious claims, although in the absence of the serious attention that the Jungians have given to religous symbolism, an omission which it may remain for future cooperation to overcome. It is only when Freudian psychology pretends to metaphysical dimensions that it becomes religiously offensive, but such presumption is not limited to psychoanalysis.

A very unusual early follower of Freud was a Swiss Lutheran pastor named Oskar Pfister. He was an enthusiastic supporter of the psychoanalytic movement, wrote a number of books and articles on its behalf, and also contributed to psychoanalytic ideas. He carried on a long correspondence with Freud, which is remarkable because it took place in a period when the relations between psychoanalysts and official representatives of religion were generally hostile.[2] My brief outline in chapter 6 of the Freudian criticism of religion will have suggested some of the reasons for this hostility. Although Freud never relented in his views about the infantile nature of religion and the need for humanity to outgrow it, he seems to have remained on the friendliest of terms with Pfister, who for his part does not appear to have deviated from his Christianity.

If anything, Pfister went too far in his enthusiasm, to the extent in one letter of calling Freud a Christian, which we may well believe did not strike Freud as accurate, and much less as a compliment.[3] Exaggeration or mere fondness aside, Pfister had a point. He grasped, as many others had not, that Freud's discoveries of human nature had revealed the primacy of love in human motivation. For all the cruelty, meanness, spite, and aggression that are so readily apparent under the masks of propriety and gentility that we wear (let alone in their too frequently unmasked forms), psychoanalysis reveals pretty convincingly that we are in search of love. It was there that Pfister saw the connection between what we might call the psychoanalytic "diagnosis" of man's condition and the Christian "diagnosis." It was another matter to call Freud "Christian" or to apply that word to his psychology, which he hoped was universal in its application. The ethic of love is not peculiar to Christianity, and it is inseparable within Christianity from a specific, historically grounded belief about God's relation to the world.

Nevertheless, there exists a profound ethical significance in a psychology that ascribes human motivation to love and its disappointments. At the very least, both practitioner and patient have to be in tacit if not explicit agreement that contrary motives, like increased power over others or other forms of unbridled egoism, whatever their short-run value, cannot be ultimately satisfying. That is, the fundamental dependence of every child on the loving environment of the family, or something like it, sets the model for all later intimacy; associated with other motives, the effort to restore this seemingly infinite care remains among the deepest of longings, to be achieved in widely differing ways. I would not want to submit that purely egocentric values do not emerge in psychoanalytic treatment and may in the end be or look like the most visible results of it, but they are not, we might say, what psychoanalysis is about.

I believe, however, that our science impinges yet more closely on Christianity. It may be that what I am going to say applies as well to all science, and also to all other forms of human interest, but let us for the moment try to think exclusively about psychoanalysis in this new context. Some time ago, writing about the contribution of psychoanalysis to religion, I took hold of a catchphrase of the time: "Question authority."[4] I tried to show how the process of psychoanalyzing is a radical questioning of ourselves, and no less of all claimants to the direction of our minds, including the analyst himself or herself. There is a kind of infinite regress in such an enterprise, and that is indeed what eventually brings an analysis to an end: when the fluidity of the logical ground is evident enough, when we come to know that our knowledge, even of ourselves, is temporal and maybe ephemeral, then it is time to stop analyzing. Perhaps the relentless questioning is also the reason why many people should not undertake analysis or cannot benefit from it: to acknowledge the bottomless uncertainty of one's existence feels to them too unsettling, maybe uncanny. But as a criticism of religious certainty and authority, the questioning is more than justified. Through it one hopes for an immediacy of faith that rests not on external authority, but on confrontation with God as he is present, in the manifold ways open to human experience. I was aware then, and am now, that this brings up further questions about organized religion, the church, and its tradition, which I shall not press at this point. What I do want to preserve from that earlier essay is the idea that psychoanalysis as an endless questioning (which I insisted must apply to the psychoanalytic theory and process, as well) can be enlisted in the service of religion, provided that it is not enlisted with the intention of doing mischief. If psychoanalysis had theological pretensions, one of them might well be the claim that questioning authority is a God-given function of the human soul.

In connection with present concerns, I want to point to a slightly different although related idea. When I discussed "concealing," I suggested that the analytic task of "unconcealing" the intentions, desires, masks, protections, and self-deceptions in which we cloak ourselves has a ring of theological familiarity to anyone who thinks about such matters. That is, our religion is a *revealed* religion; we are witnesses to a revelation, a disclosure, an unconcealment of God that took place at a particular time in a particular place and a particular manner, but also continues to take place in us. A striking rabbinical commentary on the revelation is to be found in the Mishna. According to the tradition here enshrined, Rabbi Akiba drew a telling inference from the two occasions narrated in Genesis that bear on the doctrine of the image of God in man. He said: "Beloved is man in that he was created in the image of God. Greater love was proved to him in that he was created in the image of God, as it is said: In the image of God made He man."[5]

The traditional rabbinical interpretation of these statements follows from the observation that on the second occasion God's declaration was made not to Adam, to whom of course the first refers, but to Noah.[6] That is, more than the mere creation of man in God's image, it was the imparting of the knowledge, the *disclosure* of what our true human nature consists of, that was the greater evidence of the divine love. This is what revelation is: a becoming known of what is, of being. And it is there that religion and art and science, including psychoanalysis, are at one. The difference is manifest enough: "revelation" in the theological sense means an initiative of God's; our unconcealments begin and end in human acts.[7] Nevertheless, an evidence of their kinship drawn from everyday experience is the emotion of wonder that accompanies every revelatory event. When we say "I wonder what that means?" we are led to inquire further; but the upshot of a true inquiry is yet further wonder. All investigation is exposure of the mystery that can only disclose itself. For analyst and analysand the emotion of wonder overtakes all other feeling for a while, at the contemplation of a part of the inner world that has hitherto been unexplored.

This may well seem an outlandish comparison—psychoanalysis and the divine self-disclosure—but I want to defend it as best I can. The most essential hypothesis of psychoanalysis is that we lead a life that is largely hidden from ourselves. I have discussed some of the reasons for the concealment. Note that I have said that "we lead our lives," that is, that something in our actions or our words gives evidence that our conscious intentions do not account for all we say or do. I have given a few instances of unconscious mental processes and there is no end to such examples. It often does not take an analyst to detect them; all of us do just that whenever we suspect that someone's "innocent" actions betray not-so-innocent intentions. More often than not, probably, we engage in such acts of detection defensively, or even with hostile feeling, or with a kind of triumph over the other person, but they are by no means limited to that side of our nature. When someone who is ordinarily standoffish or brusque with us "accidentally" uses an affectionate word and perhaps seems embarrassed in having done so, we may warm to that person and suspect that the earlier appearances did not represent his or her deepest feelings.

Something of the kind is the daily experience in psychoanalysis, where the acute listening of both doctor and patient is designed to permit unexpressed feelings, unformulated ideas, disregarded or lost memories, unaccepted or abandoned desires, to be spoken or to speak themselves. What is gradually learned is that self-disclosure—with the help of one who does not have the same kinds of concealment (and who knows the ones he does have) and who does not feel triumphal feelings over the weaknesses of others, avowed or not—is both liberating and innovating, and therefore creating. When we become conscious of the previously hidden ways of our minds, something new comes into being. In other words, unconcealment is also creation, just as God's work of creation and redemption is an unconcealment. Analyzing, both as doctor and as patient, is acting in the image of God.

Notes

1. S. Freud, *Letters*, selected and edited by Ernst Freud, translated by Tania and James Stern (London: Hogarth Press, 1959), p. 427.

2. S. Freud, *Psychoanalysis and Faith: The Letters of Sigmund Freud and Oskar Pfister*, ed. Heinrich Meng and Ernst L. Freud, trans. Eric Mosbacher (New York: Basic Books, 1963).

3. Ibid., letter of 29 October 1918.

4. S. A. Leavy, "Questioning Authority," *Cross Currents* 32, no. 2 (1982).

5. Pirke Aboth 3:18., in *The Ethics of the Talmud: Sayings of the Fathers*, translated and with commentary by R. T. Herford (New York: Schocken, 1945–62).

6. Genesis 9:6.

7. The concepts of unconcealment and disclosure which I have used repeatedly in this book are drawn from M. Heidegger. One statement of his that seems to me to be relevant to my position, and indeed an epitome of the psychoanalytic process, is to be found in his essay "The Origin of the Work of Art" (1935–36), in *Poetry, Language, and Thought*, trans. Albert Hofstadter (New York: Harper, 1975), p. 54: "But concealment . . . occurs within what is lighted. One being places itself in front of another being, the one helps to hide the other, the former obscures the latter, a few obstruct many, one denies all. Here concealment is not simple refusal. Rather, a being appears, but it presents itself as other than it is. . . . The unconcealedness of beings—this is never a merely existent state but a happening."

Index